Pedaling for Glory

PEDALING FOR GLORY

Victory and Drama in Professional Bicycle Racing

Samuel Abt

BICYCLE BOOKS

FROM

Motorbooks International
Publishers & Wholesalers

First published in 1997 by Motorbooks International Publishers & Wholesalers, 729
Prospect Avenue, PO Box 1, Osceola, WI 54020-0001

Motorbooks International is a certified trademark, registered with the United States
Patent Office

The information in this book is true and complete to the best of our knowledge. All
recommendations are made without any guarantee on the part of the author or
Publisher, who also disclaim any liability incurred in connection with the use of this
data or specific details

We recognize that some words, model names and designations, for example, mentioned
herein are the property of the trademark holder. We use them for identification
purposes only. This is not an official publication

Motorbooks International books are also available at discounts in bulk quantity for
industrial or sales-promotional use. For details write to Special Sales Manager at the
Publisher's address

Library of Congress Cataloging-in-Publication Data

Abt, Samuel
  Pedaling for glory : victory and drama in professional bicycle racing / Samuel Abt.
    p.   cm. — (Bicycle books)
  Includes index.
  ISBN 0-933201-83-4 (alk. paper)
  1. Bicycle racing—History.   I. Title. II. Series.
  GV1049.A287 1997   97-3485
  796.6'2—dc21

Printed in the United States of America

This book is for Steve and Christine Broening and
for George Downing and Carole Gammer, who have
all pretended for years to be interested in bicycle
racing because they knew that would please me.
Who can ask more of friends?

Acknowledgments

As always, so many people have offered support and
friendship in the reporting and writing of this book.
Among them I thank Rob van der Plas,
John Wilcockson, David Walsh, Steve Wood,
Jim Startt and Becky Rast, Beth Schneider,
Rupert Guinness, Mike Price, Tim Maloney,
Guido Roelants, Bertin de Coninck, Vincent Ronnes,
Phil Liggett, Matthew Stevenson, Philippe Van
Holle, Robert Janssens, Phil Heying, and Beth
Kozakewicz. I owe special thanks to my editors at
The International Herald Tribune and at *The
New York Times*. And, as always, my most special
thanks to my children, Claire, Phoebe, and John,
for their love.

Table of Contents

"To be understood is to be found out."
Oscar Wilde

"Me and the boys here, we've got some work to do.
You want to come along? It ain't like it used to be,
but it'll do."
Freddy Sykes, "The Wild Bunch"

Prologue: Bananas

LOOKING UP AND DOWN the Rue Général Porson, Laheycourt's main street, the man said, "It's a nice village, nice enough. Calm. Unchanged for a long time. Poor," he decided. "Poor."

The houses in sight, most of them two-story stone row houses, some of them modern tract homes, looked nice enough. But the man said he was a lifelong resident of this village in Lorraine, so he should know. A couple of other men waiting for the Tour de France to pass through said most people worked in the few steel factories still active in the area or on farms. The Tour's roads through Lorraine, in eastern France, passed one vast farm — wheat, corn, potatoes — dotted with villages dozens of kilometers apart.

"It's pretty enough here," said the gendarme blocking traffic on an approach road to the main street. He was from another village, 50 kilometers away, near Champagne. "Champagne is prettier country than Lorraine in places," he said, "and Lorraine is prettier country than Champagne in places." That seemed to sum it up for him and, looking down the road to make sure the Tour wasn't approaching, he waved some cars through.

The civic pulse beats slower in *la France profonde*, deep France, than it does in the cities. At the town hall, the most prominent notices announced a trout fishing contest in the river Chée and a lecture, with slides, about developing the memory. (There may have been other notices, but who can remember now?) Yes, all streets would be closed to traffic hours before and minutes after the Tour de France whizzed into and out of the village.

Which was why the visitors had stopped in Laheycourt. They were with the Tour and had gone ahead of the race to find food.

The village had one café and the two men seated at the bar were eating French sandwiches: a meter of bread surrounding a slice of ham thin enough to watch the Tour through. The sandwiches looked enticing to people who had not eaten since breakfast, eight hours earlier.

Two ham sandwiches. No ham sandwiches left. Two cheese sandwiches. No cheese sandwiches left. In that case, two ham and cheese sandwiches. The man behind the bar smiled.

What sandwiches were available? No sandwiches were available: There was no more bread. The day was Wednesday and the village bakery was closed. Even if it had been open, there was no more ham or cheese or sausage or lettuce or tomato or jam. Probably there never had been peanut butter or tunafish or egg salad. Don't even think BLT.

Outside, the posted menus offered, among other starters, warm goat cheese salad or the gourmet salad of greens with *foie gras* and smoked salmon. Each cost 40 francs (about $8). For a main course, choose among the fish, lotte or sandre, or try the dozen snails Alsatian style (68 francs). The slab of beef in port sauce was 75 francs. How about tagliatelles carbonara with smoked salmon (72 francs)?

Price was really no object. If it had been, the café offered pizzas, too, and onion tarts.

Everything on the menu, the man behind the bar explained, was as available as a sandwich. Which is to say, not at all. The kitchen had closed early because the Tour de France was passing through. In a few moments, the café would close entirely so that everybody could see the race. The kitchen would reopen in three hours for dinner if the visitors cared to wait. Alas, they couldn't.

They found instead a small grocery store whose stock of food, other than canned goods, was bananas. Rich in potassium, which reduces leg cramps, a banana is otherwise not as satisfying a lunch as, say, a gourmet salad with *foie gras* and smoked salmon, but it is infinitely more satisfying than the memory of breakfast.

Eating his bananas, one visitor was reminded of a story: More than a decade before, an imperious Frenchman, Jean de Gribaldy, was the *directeur sportif* of a professional cycling team that he recruited, trained, and clucked over with some success. The team, then sponsored by Sem, a manufacturer of grass seed and other agricultural wonders, was run on a small budget and won its share of small races and parts of bigger ones. But it was habitually crushed in the Tour de France by the Panasonic team, a powerhouse that operated on a much bigger budget.

Now de Gribaldy, the man said, fancied himself an expert on, among other items, riders' diets. He preferred fish to meat, for example, and insisted on small portions. He was particularly opposed to bananas as a food, feeling that they did not digest easily and sat instead on a rider's stomach for hours, slowing him in decisive sprints.

In one Tour de France, de Gribaldy's team was being overwhelmed as usual by Panasonic for all the major prizes and stages, managing only to reap crumbs. One morning, leaving their hotel they shared, members of the Sem team saw the Panasonic riders receive part of their rations for the day — the sandwiches, pastries, and sweets they would carry in the back pockets of their jerseys until they reached the halfway feed zone and received more of the same, on the flypast, in a muslin bag.

What the Panasonic riders were being given in abundance as sandwiches were long pieces of French bread with the soft white removed and replaced by bananas.

"Look, look," a Sem rider said to de Gribaldy. "We can't eat bananas, but Panasonic eats bananas."

De Gribaldy, the man said, did not skip a beat.

"Thank God," he replied. "If they didn't eat those bananas, they'd win everything in sight and there would be nothing left for us. Thank God they eat bananas."

1
Races and Faces

THE BIG BOYS, the *capos*, were up in Belgium, fighting out the Tour of Flanders over such monuments of bicycle racing as the Kwaremont, Bosberg and the Mur de Grammont hills.

There was a time when Jean-François Bernard would have been there too.

Instead, he was in the capital of Brittany the same day in 1995 for the Grand Prix de Rennes, whose greatest difficulty was the unremarkable Tabor uphill past the municipal swimming pool. Instead of the World Cup race in Flanders, Bernard was riding in the lesser Coupe de France. Instead of the big boys, the competition was Frank Hoj, a 22-year-old Dane who turned professional that year with the Collstrop team in Belgium.

"This is actually an important race for me because all the big riders are in the Tour of Flanders today," Hoj said. "So I definitely have an opportunity to show what I can do, if the conditions are right."

They weren't and he didn't, but Hoj was speaking in that golden time when anything is possible, before the start of a race. Leaning on his bicycle in the Esplanade Charles de Gaulle as 14 teams assembled, he was chatting with a fellow Danish neo-professional, 28-year-old Soren Petersen, of the Rotan Spiessens team, co-sponsor Hot Dog Louis, also based in Belgium.

Unlike Hoj, Petersen was not the competition. "This race doesn't mean so much to me," he confessed. "A good training race, because I've been sick the last two weeks. Perhaps be in the front group and do something, but mainly training."

Those words echoed Bernard's. This was only his second race of the season, which began for nearly everybody else early in February. After a winter spent looking for a job, Bernard did not get back on his bicycle until January 20. "Until then, nothing," he admitted.

He too was in the Grand Prix de Rennes for training, he said, and he too thought maybe he would do something, but mainly it was training. At age 33 that May, Jeff Bernard had been around long enough to know the rest of the cliché: "But if I can help any of my teammates, if I can help the team, of course that comes first."

When he said that, Bernard was sincere. The team always came first for him. He was a rarity, a rider who had been, and still could have been, a team leader, but who preferred to work for others. The role of team rider, the *équipier* who shelters his leader from the wind and chases down his rivals, who sacrifices his personal chances and often his wheel for a leader, suited Bernard just fine. It suits many other riders too, of course. None of them has finished third in the Tour de France, however, or been acclaimed as the next great French star.

Bernard had been so acclaimed, but that was eight years ago, before he had a terrible crash and a knee operation. Since then, he had renounced the responsibilities of a leader and the pressure the position generates. A leader is expected to win, after all. When a team labors to set him up for a victory and he cannot bag it, the leader is liable to lose respect — his own and his teammates'.

That was the problem: Bernard did not win many races. A time trial here and there, even a major time trial like the one up Mont Ventoux in the 1987 Tour, but otherwise little. His third place in the 1987 Tour was actually a comedown, since he was in the yellow jersey until he allowed an attack to trap him at the tail of the pack and conceded four minutes and the Tour.

The next three years, while he was leader of the Toshiba team, were empty. In 1988 he crashed in a badly lit tunnel during the Giro d'Italia and injured his back. The next year he developed fibrosis in his left knee and needed an operation in May and months of recuperation. In 1990, a saddle sore and another operation forced him out of the Tour de France.

In 1991 he moved to Spain to ride for Banesto, which already had two leaders, Pedro Delgado and Miguel Indurain. There was no need for a third leader, especially a Frenchman, so Bernard went as a proclaimed lieutenant, that is to say, a worker.

For four seasons he led Indurain up mountains, pacing him relentlessly until rivals — and Bernard himself — cracked. Then Indurain swooped away to victory, as leaders are supposed to do. Bernard followed, not that far behind, just enough to keep the pressure off. "I'll never be a leader," he admitted in 1993 in an interview with the sports newspaper *l'Equipe*. "I can't be someone that you can count on 100 percent, and if you ask that of me, I lose half my power."

Some suspected him of vast insecurity, others of dilettantism. A butcher's apprentice as a youth near Burgundy, he later developed a taste for expensive cars and became a collector of fine wines. He often neglected to train, preferring to spend his time hunting with friends or simply at home with his wife and two children.

Along the way with the Banesto team, he won a few races, most notably in 1992 when he was first in Paris–Nice and the Critérium International. After the 1994 season, Bernard quit Banesto. "I wanted a change of air," he explained in

Rennes. "I was there four years and it was time to change, time to come back to France, do something else, ride with a young team, take another road."

Eight teams were interested in hiring him, he continued, including such powerhouses as Polti and Motorola, and such smaller teams as Collstrop and Chazal. The problem was that Bernard insisted any new employer should also have to hire his buddy, Philippe Louviot, 31, another team worker, who was left without a team when Novémail folded.

Perhaps one of the many faxes Bernard said he received from prospective employers carried the message that only team leaders can dictate the hiring of a friend. Team workers do not enjoy that power.

Budgets were made, rosters were filled, the season began and Bernard would not waver. He and Louviot were a package. "We know each other a long time — since we were amateurs," he said in Rennes. "We rode together for Toshiba and we've been close for years. And we absolutely want to stay together."

Only Chazal, with a lust to appear in the Tour de France and a need for a rider with Bernard's name value, was willing to buy the package. An associate sponsor, an insurance company, was found to pay his and Louviot's salaries.

Despite the late start to his season, Bernard seemed unworried. "No problems at all," he said before the Grand Prix de Rennes. "My only goal is to be ready for the Tour de France, to get there in good form. Anything before then, it's not important."

He rode strongly for most of the race's 193 kilometers, dropping out with a few circuits of the city still to go. He was in Rennes just for the training, maybe to do something, maybe to help the team.

"I feel good with this team," said Bernard, the reluctant tiger. "There's no leader at Chazal. I think there are three or four riders, myself included, who are free to ride our own race. But leader? That's not what I'm looking for."

In that Tour de France, he rode invisibly but well enough to finish 34th. The next season, after a few months of minor races and no results, Bernard announced his retirement to enter the public relations business. He traveled again with the Tour, this time a civilian, and was always seen with a big smile, a lot of pals around him, and the air of a man finally freed.

Father and Son

AS ANY FATHER WOULD, Eddy Merckx offered his son a lift home from work. But Axel Merckx was delayed: "Work" had been the Het Volk bicycle race through Flanders and, on a stretch of road made slippery by heavy rain, he had crashed.

Instead of a quick shower and massage before the drive with his father to the family home outside Brussels, Axel Merckx first had to spend time visiting the Motorola team doctor. Now, as a masseur kneaded his body in a hotel room in Ghent, the younger Merckx lifted his bare legs. His shredded left knee had been cleaned and kept exposed to the air while a bloody bandage covered part of his left thigh.

"There was a small breakaway and I went after it," Axel Merckx explained. "It was during the cobblestones and I went too fast and was surprised when we came to a sharp turn." He laughed with embarrassment. "And I crashed.

"It was stupid, my fault," he said, "but racing is like that."

Sitting on a bed in the hotel room, Eddy Merckx nodded at the sentiment. No need to tell him about racing. Between them, Merckx father and son, they had 446 victories in professional races, and Eddy Merckx had 445 of them.

In his glorious career from 1965 through 1977, he won the Tour de France five times, the Giro d'Italia five times, the world championship road race three times, and the Vuelta a Espana once. Hardly a classic one-day race escaped him — three victories in Paris–Roubaix, seven in Milan–San Remo, two in the Tour of Lombardy, five in Liège–Bastogne–Liège, two in the Tour of Flanders. He broke the record for the hour's ride against the clock in 1972.

Merckx, now a bicycle manufacturer in his native Belgium, was the greatest champion the sport has known. Because of his appetite for victories, he was nicknamed "The Cannibal."

In his second full season as a professional, Axel Merckx, then 22, had that sole victory, a daily stage in the 1992 Tour de l'Avenir that he won in a sprint finish as a member of the Belgian team.

Although 1994, which he spent with the Telekom team in Germany, was a washout, his early results the next season with Motorola were promising.

Despite the crash, he finished the Het Volk in a creditable 37th place. Earlier in February, he finished 11th overall in the Trophée Laigueglia in Italy. A few days before, as the season began, he finished sixth overall in the Tour of the Mediterranean after crossing the line seventh in the testing climb up Mont Faron and 10th in an even steeper but shorter ascent in Marseille.

His strength is climbing, he explained. His father's strength was climbing, time-trialing, grinding it out for hours on the road, even sprinting — the works.

Before he turned professional, the son knew intimately how hard the sport was even for somebody not named Merckx. But he is. In bicycle-crazy Belgium, everybody knows that he is the great Eddy's son and that, so far at least, he is not the second Eddy Merckx.

Usually sons of great fathers do not try to follow in their footsteps, so why had he? Because he likes the sport, he said. Because it suits him. He played soccer at first and was good at it but decided that he could be even better at bicycle racing, which he began to do in earnest when he was 16.

"I try to do my best," Axel Merckx said, shifting on the massage table from his back to his stomach. "We'll see, year after year, if I can improve. We'll see what kind of level I can reach."

His son most resembles him, Eddy Merckx said, in character.

"He has a lot of character," the father said. "He has more character than I had. In the winter I might have had some beers with friends, but he doesn't. He likes to stay home and train a lot.

"Also he has good condition. Maybe not my power. He's very tall, so maybe not the power now. But I think in a few years he will have more power."

Axel Merckx stands 6 foot 3 inches and weighs 160 pounds. His father is a shade over 6 feet and raced at about 165 pounds.

"At the beginning he played soccer but he always said it would be cycling, so…" Eddy Merckx said. "I hope he can be a good professional. It's important in life to do what you like to do, no?"

He had not discouraged his son's choice, Eddy Merckx continued. "No," he said — a long, drawn-out "No." He searched for more words. "It was difficult to have a name like Merckx, coming after his father and being compared with the results of his father. And cyclists in Belgium always compare our results. But if he likes to do cycling, I don't see why I should say no."

Axel Merckx confirmed that it had been difficult.

"It was tough when I started in Belgium and all the guys were jealous," he said. "Now it's different. Some guys are still jealous but I'm a professional now and do my job.

"Now, in a race like today, they don't look at me as the son of Eddy Merckx. They see me as another rider, just another guy, another competitor. But maybe the guys on small teams, because I'm in Motorola and they're in a little team, they say, 'Oh why is he there and why am I on a small team?' I think I've proved I deserve the place where I am. But the jealousy, it will always live. All my life."

He hinted that his year with the Telekom team had not been happy. "It was different there. I was the only foreigner on the team, the only Belgian on a whole team of Germans." He was also sick for part of the season.

Life was much better with the Motorola team, with which he broke into the professional ranks late in 1993. "On this team there are 12 nationalities and everybody has to give a little of himself to create team morale. There's no stress here, just good feelings." Surprisingly, both Merckxs said that the father rarely offered advice about racing and that the son rarely requested it.

"Cycling has changed a lot since the time he was riding," Axel Merckx said. "And these races in Belgium, mostly I know them because I did them when I was an amateur."

Eddy Merckx echoed this, pointing out that even though he had won the Het Volk twice himself, "There's not much to tell him: Stay in front because it's all small roads and it's raining and it's dangerous. But he knows that. It's not his first year and he knows most of the races now.

"In the beginning I gave him coaching, helped train him. That's normal. But now cycling has changed so much, I can't tell him much."

If Axel Merckx had a son, would he encourage him to become a racer?

"I'd prefer not," Axel Merckx replied. "Because I know how hard it is. It may not be as hard for him as it was for me, but the name will still be following him. But if he wants to do it and likes to do it — my parents gave me the opportunity, so it's not possible that I say no to him."

Wincing, he moved off the massage table and began to dress. The injured knee, he said, would not interfere with his racing program. "One week or two for the knee to heal," he said. "For two, three days it's going to be hurting. It's not so bad."

From long experience, Eddy Merckx agreed.

"It's nothing serious," he said. "If that's all it is, it's nothing. That's part of cycling."

They began moving down the hotel corridor, heading for the car, going home. Eddy Merckx noticed that a sleeve of his son's jacket was dusty and, as any father would, reached over and brushed it off. Then his hand moved up and Eddy Merckx lovingly clapped Axel Merckx once, twice, three times on the back of the neck.

Er-os, Er-os

THE HEADY DAYS were over for Eros Poli. No more daily bouquets of summer flowers, no more crowds of young fans chanting his name. Er-os, Er-os. Ah well, Poli said.

When he mounted the podium to sign in for the 1994 Paris–Tours race, several hundred French spectators applauded politely, quietly, just as they applauded politely, quietly, all the other foreign riders. The loud cheering was reserved for French riders.

The race announcer welcomed Poli, proclaimed his victory in the Mont Ventoux stage of the last Tour de France. "A solo attack, climbed alone up the gigantic mountain, the whole pack chasing him but unable to catch him. Ladies and gentleman, the winner of the glorious Mont Ventoux stage, Eros Poli." Polite applause.

That same introduction during the Tour started a daily commotion, which became a clamor when Poli took the flowers given him as the race's most aggressive rider and, with a soft smile, passed them out. That was nearly three months earlier. Did anybody remember?

"Yeah," Poli said with enthusiasm. "One guy, before Paris–Brussels, stopped me and asked me, 'Are you Eros Poli?' Just the day before the race, I was doing some shopping, and I said, 'Yes,' and he said, 'Great, fantastic,' and asked me to sign an autograph."

The fans had dwindled but Poli did not mind. He knows who he is: an Italian rider for the Saeco team, 33 years old in 1997, a professional for six years and no star. He is a support rider, a spear carrier, and content to be who he is.

Once he might have thought he could become a star. That was in 1984, when he was one of four riders who won the gold medal for Italy in the team time trial at the Olympic Games in Los Angeles. But even as an amateur, he was usually no more than a support rider.

On the national team he worked for Mario Cipollini, the sprinter Poli had worked forall his professional career. "On the national team they asked me to prepare the sprint for Cipollini," Poli remembered. "For me it was perfect."

Blocking the wind and setting up a slipstream with his full 6 feet 4 inches, clearing rivals out with his 190 pounds, Poli is a splendid leadout man. Cipollini rides behind him for the last few kilometers, husbanding his strength, and then zips past and dashes for the line in the final few hundred meters. He wins a dozen sprints that way every season.

"I'm in this team just to work for him," Poli said. "My program is to work for him. It's very difficult to work for myself. I'm strong enough in the sprint to finish fourth, second, third but not first. And it's very important to finish first. Second is nothing. So my speciality is to help Cipollini."

After Cipollini crashed in May 1994 in the Vuelta a Espana, his head injuries and subsequent loss of balance were so serious that he had to skip both the Giro d'Italia in June and the Tour de France. The teammate who put Cipollini into the barriers, Adriano Baffi, did ride the Tour, but withdrew after a few stages. And that left Poli out of a job, as he put it, and free to seek a victory.

"For me, it's very difficult to try to win, because it's so hard for me in the mountains."

He chose a flat stage, 259.5 kilometers from Rennes to the technology theme park of Futuroscope in western France. "That was a special stage for me, no mountain, all flat; I'm not dangerous for the general classification because I'm way behind the yellow jersey, and I felt very, very strong."

He bolted away alone at Kilometer 60 and opened a huge gap. Over the silted Loire River, past vineyards and fields of wheat, through alleys of birch trees he went, building a lead that reached a maximum of 18 minutes 30 seconds at Kilometer 115. Then the pack came to life.

With 30 kilometers left, he was caught. His breakaway had lasted 166 kilometers and 4 hours. Exhausted, he finished 15 minutes behind the winner.

A few days later, he again attacked alone. This time he faced the 1,909-meter-high (6,299 feet) Mont Ventoux — 21 kilometers long on a grade of more than 8 percent for 16 kilometers and nearly 10 percent for the rest. "There it was hard. Hard. But I had 40 kilometers of descent, so that was easy."

He did not think he could last, or even get away.

"Not exactly, but I tried. I said that in the first 20 kilometers of my attack, if I could have 5 or 7 minutes' lead, I could try. Then with 100 kilometers to go, I said I could have 40 kilometers to go downhill but I have 20 kilometers to go up. So I need 20, 25 minutes." He had nearly 24, lost almost 20 of them uphill, kept most of the rest downhill and won easily after his 171-kilometer breakaway.

As a souvenir, he said, he has a photograph of the way he crossed the finish line, somehow making a sweeping bow while he pedaled. It hangs in his home in Verona.

He also has his memories. "Maybe now I know I won a big stage because now my form is not good and I remember when it was. A long year — Giro, Tour de France, 100 races. So if I go out training behind a motorbike it's very hard. Just three months ago it was so easy. Not so easy but..."

Despite the Ventoux victory, he insisted that he had no personal ambition other than to serve. So many other riders win that one big stage and start dreaming only of glory to come, but not Poli.

"No problem. I'm more popular in Italy, but that doesn't change my life. I don't feel more important, nothing special like Cipollini. He wins 10, 11 races a year; I won a stage. In the first four years I'm a professional, this is my second victory."

Absolutely nothing had changed in his head?

"No," he said quickly. Then he thought about it, his long face moving. "No, nothing." He smiled. Eros Poli was that rare being — satisfied.

A Taste of Spring

FOR MONTHS, one gray day had trudged bleakly after another. No sun, no sign of spring. Winter, still winter outside the window and inside the heart.

But not all hearts. Mario Cipollini and Gianni Bugno had tasted spring.

In the south of France, as television proved in February 1995, the bicycle racing season had begun: There was the pack, gliding along the back roads of Provence, past hills that had to be dotted with early lavender and shiny with the new leaves of olive trees. There was the sun and, when it baked the hills, there would be the scent of thyme.

The riders wore shorts and short-sleeved jerseys, the uniform of spring. Spring — Cipollini, Il Magnifico, had been waiting a while for spring. Nearly a year before, in a sprint finish in the first stage of the Vuelta a Espana, he was shouldered into a crowd barrier and crashed heavily at high speed. Because the Italian was not wearing a helmet when he thudded onto the road, he suffered a severe concussion.

Cipollini is fearless. Was fearless.

After the crash he suffered from fierce headaches and found he had lost his zest for the sprint. If he retained his speed over the final 200 meters, he no longer felt able to abandon himself to the fury of that charge. He did not get back on his bicycle for seven months.

This Tour of the Mediterranean was his first competitive race since the Vuelta. On the third stage, from Maugio to Berre among the green hills outside Marseille, Cipollini let it out, attacking with half a kilometer left. He coasted over the line, sitting up while the other sprinters were still pumping. Cipollini's long hair was blowing behind him from under his helmet and his arms were outstretched, palms down, in his familiar gesture of victory, like a holy man blessing his flock.

"Thank you, boys," he told his teammates.

Before the race finished, he recorded two more sprint victories, but the first was the best. "It was as good as winning the world championship," he said.

Bugno returned from another sort of disaster. The summer before, during the world championships in Sicily, the rumor went out that he had failed a drug test.

Not drugs exactly but caffeine, which is prohibited in extraordinary amounts as a stimulant.

Found guilty, Bugno was banned from the sport for two years under rules of the Italian Cycling Federation. On his appeal that the international laws of racing took precedence over national laws, the sentence was reduced to the standard three months.

That was not a whitewash for Bugno, who has long been a man of fragile morale and complex problems. Six years earlier, when he was still a minor rider, he began seeing a psychologist to help resolve his timidity. He also had to overcome severe vertigo, or dizziness and fear of falling when he descended a mountain at high speed. The trouble was laid to a bad crash in the 1988 Giro d'Italia and to a congenital obstruction in the canals of his inner ear. Soon an allergist found that Bugno could not tolerate wheat, milk and milk products, and changed his diet.

Retooled, Bugno became a champion, rising to the top of the computerized rankings. In the 1990 Giro he won the prologue and kept the leader's pink jersey for the rest of the race. In the Tour de France that year, he won both the climbers' big stage at Alpe d'Huez and the sprinters' at Bordeaux. In 1991 and '92 he won the professional road race championship.

The next few years had been lean, however, with only an unexpected victory in the 1994 Tour of Flanders classic to soften his decline. Everything soured: He lost confidence in his *directeur sportif*, he was divorced, he moved from Italy to Monaco. The positive drug finding and the two-year ban confronted Bugno, at age 31, with the probability that his career was through.

Like Cipollini, the Tour of the Mediterranean was the first race of the season for Bugno. On the next to last stage he worked hard to spring a young MG teammate, Davide Rebellin, off and away on the nine-kilometer Mont Faron climb near Toulon. When Rebellin could not shake a rival, Bugno overtook them both and swept to victory himself. Wiping the sweat from his face, he stood in the sun and said he hoped this victory would simply be the first of many.

The next day, the sun moved from Provence to Paris and the street market was suddenly full of flowers: crocus, pygmy iris, narcissus, primula in all the colors of the rainbow jersey. Down south it was dark and overcast.

The Tour of the Mediterranean ended in the streets of Marseille with a climb up the Notre Dame de la Garde hill, 550 meters long and a grade of 20 percent. Like the Mont Faron ascent, this was asking a lot of riders early in the season and few were up to it. Bugno zipped to another easy victory, both the stage and the overall.

Because he wore only the slightest smile, he might have seemed remote, even indifferent, when the television cameras moved in afterward and the questions began. His answers were banal.

As Bugno knew, for weeks to come, a bright sun would be exceptional. Prudence and caution were called for. Down in Provence, it felt like spring but was still winter.

Waiting in the Rain

THE RACING SEASON opened on the northern front, moving from the temperate breezes of the Riviera and Andalusia to the stinging cold and daylong drizzle of Belgium.

"The rain is no problem, not for Belgian riders," said Eddy Planckaert, formerly one of those riders and a distinguished one. Sitting in the comfort of the Bloso Sports Center in Ghent, Planckaert was discussing the Het Volk race, which he won in 1984 and '85. "It's the most beautiful race of the beginning of the year," he said. "If you win, you have a lot of publicity, as much as if you win a classic."

The Het Volk, which was first organized in 1945 by the Flemish newspaper of that name, is a classic — an important one-day race — but not a *classic* classic, not a great one-day race, not one of the 11 classics that compose the World Cup, and not a classic that means much outside Belgium.

"For a Belgian rider, a victory here means he's got a job for next season," said Claude Criquielion, another formerly distinguished Belgian rider. "No matter how well he does the rest of the year, a victory here wins him a new contract. That's how important the race is to the Belgian people. For everybody else," Criquielion admitted, "it's not a very big race."

But if the Het Volk's meaning is narrow, it is profound.

"For a Belgian sponsor especially," explained Jean-Luc Vandenbroucke, the *directeur sportif* of the Lotto team and yet another formerly distinguished Belgian rider, second in the Het Volk in 1984 and third in 1981. He was surrounded by dozens of fans, who were standing content in the cold rain and gazing at bicycles and riders as teams began arriving for the race. "It's very important to win the Het Volk because it's the start," Vandenbroucke continued. "The Belgian people have waited impatiently for the season to start and here it is."

Belgian fans, among the most intense in Europe, had been waiting for more than their season to start, three weeks after the campaign began in Spain, Italy, and southern France. Since the great Eddy Merckx retired 20 years earlier, those fans had been waiting for another Belgian champion, some rider swift and voracious enough to show the world how rock-hard Belgians can be and how triumphant. Instead, the fans had to settle for Planckaert, Criquielion and Vandenbroucke, among others. Respected riders, winners all, but not one a great champion. Those three are retired now. The new Eddy Merckx is still slouching toward Brussels, waiting to be born.

In Ghent, inside the sports center, riders were entering rooms to change into racing uniforms while hundreds of fans wandered the corridors. Bicycle racing is an immediate sport — fans are not held back from the athletes by long lines of policemen but are allowed to mingle, to seek autographs, to exchange a few words with the riders before and after a race.

For many Belgian riders, this was as close as they would come to big-time adulation. The Het Volk attracted 24 teams of 8 riders each and some of those teams were the minor, small-budget ones that usually appear only in Belgian and

Dutch kermesses, insignificant criterium races through and around villages to break the torpor of a weekend.

Asfra, Palmans, Zetelhallen, Cedico, Tonissteiner Saxon, Vlaanderen 2002, Espace Card, Hot Dog Louis: Who outside Belgium had heard of these teams? Here they were, competing against such giants as Mapei, Motorola, Festina, Gan, Castorama, Polti, Novell, Lotto and Le Groupement. Those were the teams that would go on to all the races, the *classic* classics, that are closed to the Asfras and Espace Cards.

Over the hall's public address system came an announcement for the fans to please stop blocking the corridors. A few young children looked tentatively at their fathers, who shrugged and continued to point out the gearing of this bicycle and the fork rake of that one. Not until the riders began leaving the sports center did the fans follow.

The rain was pelting his Brescialat team car as Eric Vanderaerden spilled from a bag six or eight small sandwiches and pastries, each wrapped in tin foil, and began packing them into the back pockets of his jersey.

A decade before, he had been another new Eddy Merckx, a feared sprinter, an excellent rider of short time trials. Then he lost just enough power and ambition and gained just enough age to become no more than another respected Belgian rider. He was in his mid-30s and his face had lost its sleek look in a web of deep lines.

Third in the Het Volk in 1992 and '93, Vanderaerden had little pressure on him this time. "I'm with an Italian team now, so this race is not so important to me," he said. "I hope to do my best, no more." His goals for the rest of the season were equally limited. "To win something. Last year I didn't win a race, so I hope to do it this year."

It didn't happen in the Het Volk. Somewhere during the 205-kilometer race past Flanders' waterlogged fields, through sodden villages and over 11 steep, slickly cobblestoned hills, Vanderaerden dropped out. So did many others in the 192-man field. Eighty-five riders made it to the end back in Ghent, with 39 more finishing but being disqualified because they were outside the time limit.

Despite its tiring hills and winter weather, the Het Volk is often decided in a sprint finish. This day, however, three riders broke away at Kilometer 55, on the climb up the Oude Kwaremont, and managed to stay away, aided by a passing train that kept the chasing pack blocked at a railway crossing for two minutes.

For a Belgian fan, the three riders represented a problem in loyalties. One was indeed Belgian — Edwig Van Hooydonck, second in the Het Volk in 1990 and third the next year — but he rode for the Novell team based in the Netherlands. Another in the breakaway — Andrei Tchmil — rode for the Belgian Lotto team but was Russian. The third was no problem at all: Franco Ballerini, an Italian who rode for the Mapei team in his homeland.

Ballerini proved to be the strongest. In the final few kilometers, with the pack half a minute behind, the Italian attacked three times and twice was caught by Van Hooydonck and Tchmil. They could not respond the third time. By six seconds and about 200 meters, Ballerini was so clearly the winner that he had time to applaud his performance and straighten his jersey before he coasted across the line with his arms upraised. He became only the fifth foreigner in half a century to win this most beautiful of Belgium's early season races. Belgian fans would have to wait at least another year to cheer in the rain for one of their own.

Little Mig's Big Dreams

BIG MIG HAD GOALS, such as winning his fifth successive Tour de France, to match his nickname. So did Little Mig, such as completing the 1995 race and maybe, just maybe one day, crossing a finish line with the main group.

Not winning the stage, understand. Little Mig knew his limits. He simply wanted to share the thrill of being one of the first 10 or 15 riders across. Even the first 20 or 25, as long as they were in the first group. Whatever the number, the first group is called the leaders.

Guess which Mig — Miguel Indurain, the Spaniard who rode for the Banesto team and wore the yellow jersey that July, or Miguel Arroyo, the Mexican who rode for the Chazal team and wore the Chazal jersey — was closer to fulfilling his goals?

Sigh. Indurain had spent the previous week propelling his 6-foot-2-inch, 174-pound frame across the finish line in first, second and third places. He was leading the Tour by nearly three minutes and would win it by nearly five.

In 59th place — 1 hour 40 minutes 35 seconds behind — stood the 5-5, 130-pound Arroyo. He would finally finish in 61st place among the 115 riders left, almost 2 hours 20 minutes behind Indurain.

"The pace is so fast, too fast for me," Arroyo said while the race was still on the flat. It was indeed fast then, more than 40 kilometers an hour. A few days later it was about 5 kph slower, but there were some big mountains to get over: two climbs rated fourth category, the lowest in length, steepness and general difficulty, two rated third, one rated second, and one rated first. In a horde of riders, 28:5 behind the winner, Arroyo arrived in 59th place.

If only he could do better, he said. He was doing his best: a veteran of the ADR, Z and Subaru teams, then in his second year with Chazal and a transplant in 1996 to the ForceSud team, the Mexican has always ridden to his maximum potential when the climbing began. "It's so important to the team for me to do something in the mountains," Arroyo said.

For the second successive year, his Chazal team had been allowed into the Tour on sufferance. It was a low-budget French team and the publicity it engendered in the Tour for its sponsor, a wholesale vendor of cold cuts, was all that stood between it and extinction. No Tour, no spurt in the sale of salami, no team. The race organizers understood this and felt a special responsibility to a French team.

By the same logic, Arroyo, Chazal's best climber, was not the team leader. "No, it's Jean-François Bernard," he said, referring to the French rider who not only had seen better decades but also had announced that he was leaving Chazal the next season for a new French team.

Under Bernard, Chazal had scored exactly one victory so far that season. It happened in a minor race not long before the Tour, and just after the team was warned by the Tour's organizers that their invitation might be withdrawn unless Chazal riders started showing results worthy of an entry.

"Maybe in the mountains I'm the leader," Arroyo said. "It's a big responsibility. My form is good. I finished seventh in the Dauphiné, and in the mountains there I finished with Indurain and Richard Virenque."

Not in this Tour, though. In the first Alpine stage, the Mexican was 45th, 19:01 behind Indurain, and nearly 15 minutes behind Virenque, who was wearing the polka-dot jersey of the Tour's top climber. The next day, Arroyo finished 52nd into Alpe d'Huez, 15:25 behind Indurain and 13:31 behind Virenque. And the day after that, as the Alps were finished with, he was nearly 25 minutes behind Indurain and 23 behind Virenque.

In the big picture, the Chazal team had been equally undistinguished, ranking 16th among the 21 Tour entries in total elapsed time. In prizes, Chazal had won 31,500 francs (about $6,200) as compared with the 579,550 francs for the ONCE team atop the standings.

Ordered by their *directeur sportif*, Vincent Lavenu, to display the team jersey and move some garlic sausage, the riders were semi-visible during the first week on the flat in Brittany, northern France and Belgium. Especially were they to be seen after 3:15 P.M., when French television usually begins its daily Tour coverage.

Since then, however, in the Alps, the long and difficult stages in the Massif Central and then the Pyrenees, Chazal had entered a Bermuda Triangle. The team had not cut the mustard, let alone caused it to be spread on the sponsor's mortadella.

Arroyo was on a mission. He had two stages left in the Pyrenees to finish with the leaders and blaze his team's name into the nation's delicatessens. Could he do it? It was doubtful. This job called not for somebody as modest and soft-spoken as Arroyo, but for a real hot dog.

Amateur's Hour

HERE HE IS, full of hope, in Isbergues, the north of France, nowhere — a company town, 5,500 inhabitants, a couple of streets, no evident restaurant, a half-mile walk from the nearest train station. For Cyril Sabatier, Isbergues is Carthage under Hannibal, Athens in the Golden Age of Pericles.

Isbergues is where it all could happen.

Maybe, maybe not.

Sabatier was lying on his back on the massage table, wearing a gray Gan T-shirt. A towel was draped over his middle as a *soigneur* worked on his legs. Sabatier had flown up that morning from his home in Nimes, been met at the airport in Paris by a Gan team official and then driven to a hotel in the city of Béthune. The next day he would begin his four-race internship with the team.

Every fall, the French Cycling Federation encourages the country's handful of professional teams to accept up to three amateurs for a stage, a few weeks of experience at a higher level and the opportunity to impress team officials enough so that they will sign the amateur rider to a two-year neo-professional contract.

Once in a while, that happens. Of the 109 French riders who started the 1995 season with professional teams, 30 were neo-pros. This figure was skewed, however, since 12 of them were with promotional, or second-division, teams and 6 with Le Groupement, a team that disappeared, along with their jobs, in mid-season.

Most of these amateurs were signed to a professional contract based on their results, not their stage, which is often a token last chance. Usually the amateur — the *stagiaire* — rides his races and then returns to his amateur team, humbled. Next season, he pledges, he will ride so well that he will not need a stage to win a professional contract.

Sabatier did not think he would be saying that. He was 24 years old then, a little old to remain a hopeful amateur, dreaming about next season's results.

"If it doesn't work out this season, I think it's over for me," he said as he rolled onto his side for the massage. "It's too hard to stay an amateur — not enough teams, not enough money. Another year as an amateur? I don't think so, I don't think so. This is my last chance, I know that."

He was nervous, he admitted. "Yes, a little, yes." Tired too. "A little of that also, yes. It's been a long season." The champion of France among cadets, age 12, and then among juniors, age 16, Sabatier had not continued to shine these last several seasons. He did win the unheralded Tour du Nivernais-Morvan that year and did finish fourth in the amateur Liège–Bastogne–Liège, but otherwise his results had been undistinguished.

The week before he had dropped out of the Tour de l'Avenir, a showcase for young talent, during an early stage. Was that race too hard, the weather too brutal? "I was too tired," he explained now. "I wanted to save what I have left for these races with Gan."

A team official was pessimistic about Sabatier. "His chances — nothing special," the official said.

"He's a good rider but tired now," said another official, Michel Laurent, the Gan manager. "He's had some good results, nothing extraordinary, but he's solid. He's getting his opportunity to impress us." Still, Laurent added, "At most we'll take one neo-pro and we're looking at three. Perhaps we won't take any of them."

Those were bad times for French teams. Both Castorama and Chazal were seeking financial backing to continue in 1996 and Castorama never did find it. The only French teams assured of resuming action the next February were Gan, the minor-league Aubervilliers 93 and Mutuelle de Seine et Marne outfits, and Festina, which was then based in Andorra. Two other second-division teams, La Creuse and ForceSud, were in the talking stage.

"There aren't many French teams, that's sure," Sabatier said. "I contacted Gan, that's why I'm here.

"In Italy, they'll have 12 teams next season. I don't know anybody there, though, so I've had no contact with Italian teams.

"This stage — it's a big opportunity. I know that. Maybe my first big opportunity and I know I have to take advantage of it."

Exactly how remained to be worked out. "I don't know what my goals are because I've never done a big race with professionals. I have no idea what's expected of me tomorrow, not yet," he said, referring to the Grand Prix d'Isbergues, his first race with Gan. "Nobody has told me anything yet. I'll find out what they want me to do later."

Finishing the 206-kilometer race over 13 short yet steep climbs was foremost on his mind. "I certainly hope to finish. That would be good for me with the team."

Actually, no, Laurent said later. "Personal results don't mean much with a young rider," he explained, "because we may ask him to do so many things that he wears himself out. I don't hold it against a young rider if he doesn't finish, as long as he does the team's work and that's why he dropped out.

"What I look for is whether he gets in the early breaks, does he work for the others, does he do his share of the chasing, does he ride for the leaders, giving them shelter from the wind? An individual exploit is always admirable — it certainly can't hurt your chances — but the rest counts just as much.

"What you want to know is how will a young rider fit in, how good is his attitude. Sometimes a rider's legs are terrific but his head isn't."

Laurent mentioned a French professional of great promise but lackluster recent results. "He can't focus on training and racing," the manager charged. "He gets distracted. Family problems, personal problems. Girls. He's supposed to be thinking about training and racing and what's he thinking about? Women."

Married and a father, Sabatier appeared to be distant from that problem. He had his own, although it was in the past. In July 1988, the month of his 17th birthday, he was found guilty of using steroids when he won the French junior championship a few weeks before. His title was removed.

His father fought the positive drug finding for more than two years, arguing with a thick dossier of medical reports that his son naturally produced an excessively high level of testosterone, the natural male hormone, and an abnormally low level of epitestosterone, a natural precursor of testosterone. A ratio between the two higher than 6 to 1 is considered proof of doping and the young Sabatier routinely registered a ratio of at least 8 to 1.

In 1990, the boy was finally cleared and his title restored. Had the years of testimony and doubt sapped his powers, or was Sabatier simply another case of the young rider who never lived up to his potential? However delicately it could be put, that was not a question to ask a rider thinking only of his stage with Gan. In any case, he said, he had not tested positively in years and probably had outgrown whatever glandular condition he had as a teenager.

"That part's over, finished," he was saying. "What I have to think about now is the Grand Prix d'Isbergues first, then a couple of races in Italy, then

Paris–Bourges, I think. That's my stage, my opportunity. Everything depends now on my legs."

How were his legs? "We'll find out tomorrow," he answered.

And if he failed in his stage, what then?

"I don't know," he said, "I haven't even thought about it. For now this is all I'm thinking about. We'll see next year what I'm doing next year."

The next morning, when he showed up at the team car to head for the Grand Prix d'Isbergues, Sabatier's Gan racing jersey and shorts were shinily new and spotless, obviously just out of the box. The bicycle locked atop the car, however, was his usual one. The only difference was the number 28 bolted onto it for the race.

"There's no time to measure him for a new bicycle and build one," explained a Gan mechanic. "He just got here and he'll only be with us for four races, a couple of weeks."

So, for the first racing day of his stage, Sabatier rode the familiar yellow Peugeot bicycle he used with the amateur VC–Lyon– Vaulx en Velin team. Also on a yellow Peugeot was Anthony Langella, a 21-year-old member of the CC Marmande-Aquitaine team, another amateur *stagiaire*. His number was 25. The seven other Gan riders, all professionals, rode blue Eddy Merckx models.

Sabatier and Langella were driven from their hotel in Béthune to Isbergues, about 20 kilometers away, by Laurent. After a team meeting that morning, during which the manager outlined strategy and general duties, he took the opportunity of the drive to give the amateurs some last-minute advice.

"Tactics," he said, "pay attention to tactics, stay alert, take advice from the other riders. Stay alert. There should be lots of attacks, early attacks, so stay alert. Follow the attacks, pay attention to tactics. Listen to the others." Laurent spoke mainly to Langella, in the front seat with him, but turned now and again to Sabatier to make sure he did not feel ignored.

Looking grim and a bit nervous, Sabatier kept nodding his head in agreement with everything Laurent told him. Tactics. Stay alert.

The team drove in three cars to the small town of Isbergues for its 49th Grand Prix bicycle race. Started in 1946 to celebrate France's liberation from the Germans the year before, the Grand Prix is sponsored by the Ugine factory, the only one in town, which advertises itself as the world's leading manufacturer of stainless steel for cutlery. Secondary sponsors include the Pas de Calais region in which Isbergues sits, just off the main road north to Calais and Dunkirk, happily out of sight of the numerous hills of slag that show where coal once was mined.

The countryside in the north of France is not the stuff of picture postcards and the people tend to be thick and lumpy, with prominent Punch and Judy chins. The weather is generally windy because of the nearby English Channel and rain is common. That morning started in heavy fog that was now beginning to be burnt off.

Once he arrived, Sabatier waited for a *soigneur* to oil his legs for warmth, then rode to the race podium to sign in. Unlike many of the riders, he received no introduction — clearly the speaker had no idea who he was. Even if it is part of the Coupe de France competition, the Grand Prix d'Isbergues is a secondary race and does not waste its money (66,000 francs — about $13,000 then — in prizes) on a professional introducer of riders.

"There's nothing special about this race," explained Brian Holm, a Dane who usually rides at a higher level for the Telekom team based in Germany. For the Grand Prix he was part of a mixed entry comprising riders whose teams sent only a man or two.

Why was he here then? "I like to race Isbergues because I lived here when I was an amateur," he said. "I get to see people I know. The race is hard but nothing much to win."

Nevertheless it attracted more than 150 riders divided among 19 teams, including such major ones as Lotto, Gan, Motorola, Novell and Castorama, and such minor ones as Saxon, Rotan, Palmans, Asfra and Vlaanderen 2002. There was room for anybody applying, since the Spanish teams were all busy that weekend in the Vuelta a Espana and the Italian teams were racing on their home front.

Unsung, Sabatier started to leave the podium area when a photographer — one with a press badge, not simply a fan — asked him to pose. He obliged. Then a spectator asked for an autograph. Looking pleased, Sabatier signed with his left hand.

He pedaled over to the riders' tent, where he could have some coffee or a piece of bread. Sitting on his bicycle with his sunglasses perched on his head, his right leg on the ground for balance, Sabatier gazed out at the spectators on the other side of the barriers.

He seemed happy. Perhaps he was registering the amateur riders out there, the ones in unknown team jerseys or in those of Banesto and Festina, professional teams not entered in the Grand Prix d'Isbergues. Perhaps those were the men who caught his eye, the pretenders, the dreamers, the young riders who stood there admiringly and wished, like him, that one day they would turn professional.

An official tapped Sabatier on the shoulder and nodded to the right. He rode off to the start of his first professional race.

Whatever fine feats he accomplished went unseen. Heeding tactics, covering early breaks, listening to the advice of his teammates, staying alert, especially staying alert — whatever he did after the first 30 kilometers went unseen because his Gan team leader, Gilbert Duclos-Lassalle, attacked successfully with two Lotto riders and began to build a huge lead.

Naturally, the team car with Laurent at the wheel went with Duclos to offer advice, inspiration, a water bottle or a new wheel if he had a flat.

Unlike a major race, where teams have two cars, one to tend a breakaway, one for the rest of the team in the pack, the Grand Prix d'Isbergues had one car for each team. If that car went up front, wheels and water bottles for the other riders were provided by a neutral support car.

Undoubtedly Sabatier worked with his teammates to protect Duclos. But there was no Gan official there to see his work and judge how he would fit into the team the next season.

No matter. Like so many other riders, Sabatier ran out of steam after a majority of the 13 hills. Perhaps it was all the crashes on the narrow, twisty roads that 150 riders were trying to barrel through. More likely it was what he feared, that after a long season, he was just too tired to finish the race. Langella, his fellow amateur, did finish, however.

Later, after Sabatier had showered and returned to the team car to be driven back to the hotel to pack his bags and head for the two races in Italy, he was asked what had happened to him in the Grand Prix d'Isbergues.

"No, I didn't crash," he said. "I just ran out of strength on a hill and had to quit." He was working not to look disheartened, not to acknowledge that in the next two weeks of his stage he would not grow any stronger than he had been here.

A team mechanic came up and asked him if he had pulled out because of a crash.

"No," Sabatier explained, "I didn't crash. "I just ran out of strength on a hill and had to quit," he repeated, trying hard to sound matter of fact and not succeeding, not at all.

2

Welcome to China

IT'S A GREAT PLACE for bargains, for sure. "I don't want to say I just came here for the shopping and the vacation," Max Sciandri said, smiling sheepishly because he had just admitted that, as quickly as he could say "duty free," he had bought a camera in the few hours since he arrived in Hong Kong.

"Good selection here and you can bargain prices, not like Europe," he continued. "You say, 'Too high' and start to leave, and they grab you by the sleeve and lower the price."

Then he turned dutiful. "It's going to be an interesting race," he said, referring to the first Tour of China race. "Interesting and maybe unpredictable."

Sciandri, then a 28-year-old Italian (in a few months, to ensure that he rode in the Olympic Games in Atlanta, he became a 28-year-old Briton), had to postpone the rest of his analysis of the 11-day, 500-kilometer race that was staged in November 1995. "More shopping," he confessed. "But I'll be all business for the race once it starts."

Luckily for him, the first Tour of China, which was sponsored by Kent cigarettes, did not begin for another day. That should have left the morning free for a visit to any of the thousands of shopping emporiums, all boasting half-price sales.

A 310-mile race, roughly two long daily stages in the Tour de France, did not sound like an ordeal able to be spread over 11 days from Hong Kong to Beijing. The organizers had scheduled extremely short stages most days and left plenty of time in between for long transfers by bus and plane.

First listed was a 2.8-kilometer prologue in the Shatin district near the Royal Hong Kong Jockey Club race track. Fifteen teams, amateurs and professionals, would send out seven men each in the race against the clock. The next day, the

29

Tour crossed the border into China, staging a 55-kilometer road race at Shenzhen, and then traveled to Guangzhou for a 145-kilometer race, the longest scheduled. After two days off for travel and rest, if any was needed, the race would resume in Shanghai with a 70-kilometer circuit race. The day after that would see another circuit race in Shanghai, this time over 76 kilometers. Then two more travel and rest days would carry the Tour to Beijing for a 132-kilometer road race to the Great Wall and a 25-kilometer concluding time trial in the city.

Most riders thought the two stages in Beijing would decide the winner.

"Both the fifth stage, which has some climbing, and the time trial should be hard, but I think the fifth stage to the Great Wall will be decisive," said Daniele Nardello, an Italian with the Mapei team and the second-place finisher in the esteemed Tour of Lombardy the weekend before. He was a favorite in the Tour of China, a status he shared with Slava Ekimov, a Russian with the Novell team; Gianni Bugno, an Italian with the MG team; perhaps even Djamolidine Abdoujaparov, an Uzbek with Novell; and Sciandri, who rode for MG that year, before he moved to Motorola in 1996.

All were big names in the sport, as were their teams. Other big professional outfits in this Tour included Castorama from France, Collstrop from Belgium, and Saturn and U.S. Postal Service from the United States. How did Medalist Offshore, the organizers, and British-American Tobacco, the sponsors through its Kent brand, lure them to the debut of a race at the end of the season, when riders are exhausted?

The answer, as always, was money. The organizers, many of the same people who stage the Tour DuPont in the United States, learned years ago that a prize list two or three times higher than most European races will attract teams. A total of $200,000 would be available in prizes, with $50,000 going to the winner and $30,000 to the runner-up. A stage victory would be worth $2,500.

That was one factor, said Michael Plant, the executive director of the race. He also stressed the benefits to Asians in watching their first professional stage race and being "able to see world-class athletes up close."

Steve Hegg, an American with the USPro team and the 1984 Olympic pursuit champion, agreed that the race would be worthwhile.

"The word is that it will be very interesting, very different," he said. "The shortness of the stages, the lateness of the season will make it different. Speed is going to be a big factor." Hegg discounted reports that China's roads, often unpaved and corrugated, would be a handicap. "They can't be any worse than training in traffic anywhere in the world."

Plus, as Sciandri could have told him, there was all that duty-free shopping.

Ekimov admitted that he had brought his wife with him, virtually unheard of at a bicycle race. "She wanted to come on vacation," he explained.

Did he too? "No, no," he protested. "I have a good opportunity to win this race and any race I can win is important to me. For me this is no vacation. It's work."

Hong Kong's Elite

MAN WAI-CHUNG, the 19-year-old junior cycling champion of Hong Kong, shook his head slowly sideways in the universal word for no when he was asked if he ever hoped to become a professional. Asked why not, he spread his hands far apart.

"Too great a distance between him and the professionals," explained Charles Chow, the technical adviser to the seven-man amateur Hong Kong team in the first Tour of China. Man, who insisted that he spoke little English, nodded in agreement, saying something softly to Chow. "He just hopes to become one of the best amateurs," Chow translated. "He already is in Hong Kong."

Bicycle racing is a popular sport in Hong Kong, Chow continued, with about a dozen amateur clubs competing. The Hong Kong Cycling Association reported that it had 200 riders and 30 to 35 officials. The season lasts from October to May, avoiding the summer heat and typhoons. Because the roads are so jammed with cars, races usually start at 6:30 A.M. on Sundays and end four hours later. Man had already won more than his fair share of those races, Chow said.

Then, riding in the short prologue, Man showed that for this day at least the distance between him and the professionals was not that great at all. While he placed 96th in the 110-man field, he was the second fastest on the Hong Kong team, and finished a creditable 47 seconds behind the winner.

First was Steve Hegg, who was clocked in 5 minutes 2 seconds over the 4.1-kilometer course, which was lengthened from the scheduled 2.8 kilometers at the last moment. Second, in 5:05, was Daniele Nardello and third, in 5:09, was Norm Alvis, an American with Saturn. Hegg described the course in the Shatin district as "ideal, rider friendly" because "it wasn't technical, it was easy to learn, you didn't have to remember where that pothole was." The weather was balmy under an overcast sky that began to sprinkle toward the end.

A small but lively bunch of spectators, many of them in the jerseys of European professional teams, turned out for the start. They were outnumbered by the drivers who sulked in their cars as unsmiling policemen blocked the roads — a Tour de France scene, except that, unlike France, nobody dared honk. Decorum on the circuit was perfect, except when a middle-aged man on a clunker of a bicycle gaily rode up the road, waving to one and all, as the last entrants were bearing down on him from the other direction. When there was no crash, the incident passed as just one of those things.

Man was a popular figure, signing autographs and answering fans' questions, as he waited for his turn to start.

"A nice boy and a good rider, maybe second or third best in Hong Kong," said Ernest Law, the head of the medical control, or doping test, for the International Cycling Union at the race. Law, also an official of the Hong Kong Cycling Association, patted Man on the back as he moved to the starting ramp.

His day will come, Chow said earlier as Man ducked his boyish face in embarrassment at the prediction. "He's a long-distance rider and a good climber,"

Chow continued, "and if he makes it to the fifth stage, the one to the Great Wall and the climbs before, he should do well."

That "if," both of them agreed, was the point. "He's afraid of the speed the race may reach," Chow explained. "He's afraid it may go too fast."

His best, Man said, was 50 to 55 kilometers an hour for a few minutes, a good pace for somebody his age. "I can't stay there long," he said. "He's a long-duration rider but he's too young to stay fast for the long duration," Chow added.

Man said that his main goal was to make it to the finish in Beijing, the time trial a day after the slog to the Great Wall. But if Man did not make it that far — he eventually did — he said he still expected many benefits. "I want to learn how professionals ride, when to attack, how to chase, when to change gears." So much to learn in 10 days, he agreed. "He's very willing," Chow said, "and he's been in big races before."

In fact, he had returned a few weeks before from the world championships in Colombia, where he lasted about halfway through the amateur road race. Not many riders got that distance in the thin air and testing conditions in Colombia, and even fewer were just 19 years old.

He had also raced in the United States and expected to make a European tour, four to six weeks long, the following spring with his Ngan Hin club team. For training, Man went out daily in the New Territories, where the prologue was staged, and rode about 100 kilometers. The rest of his time was spent on a motorcycle, delivering express mail.

Man said he had been racing since he was 13 or 14 years old. What had drawn him to the sport was noticing a bicycle race go by and seeing how glorious the riders looked in their multicolored jerseys and how strong they all seemed.

That was exactly what attracted Greg LeMond to the sport when he watched his first bicycle race go by at about the same age, Man was told. He knew who LeMond was, and he knew that he had won the Tour de France three times. His boyish face broke into a big smile, and this time Man shook his head slowly up and down in the universal word for yes.

Across the Border, Finally

IN THE END, almost everybody agreed, it was the Kazakhs' fault. Definitely. Not the Italians' and not the Belgians' either.

The only dissenters might have been the Kazakhs themselves, the seven-man team in the Kent Tour of China and their handful of mechanics and officials. But who was listening to them? Who spoke Kazakh other than the Kazakhs?

Certainly not the Chinese border guards — the friendly men and women in the green uniforms of the army, and the scowling men in the white uniforms of the police, bearing enough gold braid on their caps and shoulder boards to humble the chairman of the U.S. Joint Chiefs of Staff. Somebody in that group — or perhaps it was the nervous man in the sharkskin suit on the bus who looked like a police undercover agent and, the rumor mill said, turned out to be a police undercover agent — decided that the Kazakhs' visa was irregular.

Not exactly irregular, the rumors had it, but sort of Russian. Since the breakup of the evil empire, Kazakhstan has been an independent country, but before that — well...

And everybody knows how the Chinese feel about the Russians, or are supposed to feel about them, or used to feel about them. (In fact, the language barrier was not that great since fair-skinned Kazakhs, the bulk of the team, speak Russian, but that surely would have confirmed suspicions.) Perhaps it really was true, as the first rumor had it, that two riders, no, make that four riders, did not have Chinese entry visas. No, make that the entire Mapei team from Italy and the entire Collstrop team from Belgium, who did not have individual visas, but each did have one sheet of a collective visa that was not acceptable to somebody in a green or a white uniform or even a sharkskin suit.

Or something.

In any case, the entry of the Tour of China into China was delayed for nearly two hours at the border with Hong Kong after the departure of the race from Hong Kong was delayed more than an hour on the other side of the border. Exit and entry forms were the problem, the rumors said.

Time passed in a jovial way at both stops, with people being told to pile off their four yellow double-decker buses and then immediately being told to please, please, get back on the buses. At one point in China the dozen accompanying journalists were told to leave their buses with their baggage, which did wonders to uplift the mood of the many representatives of the race's sponsors and advertisers aboard. Once down, the journalists were told to please, please get right back up. A mischief maker re-entered his bus and announced that the authorities had decided instead to round up all petty bourgeois elements, namely businessmen, for re-education clinics. Just joking, folks.

The crossing point was at Shenzhen, a Special Economic Zone, which is often written with the "S" in "Special" barred vertically into a dollar sign.

The business of Shenzhen, a charmless collection of skyscrapers, building sites and corrugated tin sheds, is, what else?, business. As the buses carrying the Tour of China entourage sat first on one side of the frontier and then the other, members could notice a reversal of stereotypes: on the Hong Kong side, meadows and fish ponds; on the China side, a horizon full of high-rises and the national bird of China, the crane, as in building crane.

Of course, the Tour of China did make it across, speeding through the city with a police escort. The buses pulled in to the Shenzhen Sports Complex, a huge soccer stadium, more or less on schedule, a good two hours before the riders began the first stage. Somebody seemed to have anticipated a bit of delay at the border.

And the first stage of the first professional bicycle race in the Middle Kingdom began on time too, 2 P.M. Shenzhen Sports Complex time. Fifty-five kilometers and 1 hour 18 minutes 22 seconds later, the stage ended in a victory by Damien Nazon, a French sprinter with the Castorama team, which, unlike Shenzhen, was going out of business at the end of the year. A lot Nazon cared. He was planning to sign with the Banesto team in Spain, led by Miguel Indurain and heretofore lacking a fine sprinter. Nazon, then 21 and until a few weeks before an amateur, was their boy.

He proved that by beating one of the better sprinters around, Djamolidine Abdoujaparov, an Uzbek, whose name was as unpronounceable to the Chinese announcer as it was to the American one. Third was Robbie Ventura, an American with the USPro team. The pack of 104 riders crossed the line mainly in the same time as Nazon, and Steve Hegg continued to wear the leader's yellow jersey that he won in the prologue.

The race finished at the Mission Hills Golf Club, a decidedly palatial sprawl. Several hundred people, some in elegant golfers' clothes and some wearing the conical straw hat of the peasant, gathered there to watch in mild weather.

Parts of the route, a sleek new expressway that was closed to all traffic but the Tour of China's, were also lined with crowds. Racing at the amateur level is a somewhat popular sport in China, where the bicycle is more commonly used as a means of transportation for people and goods.

In Shenzhen, at least, cars did not seem to be rare, but they were not plentiful either. Each of the 15 teams had a car for its own use in the race and some were requisitioned taxis with their meters hooded. The oldest appeared to be the vehicle given to the Saturn team from the United States, which showed more than 725,000 kilometers on its odometer. That would have to be turned back to a respectable 600,000 kilometers before the car was sold in the next decade or two.

'It's Real'

ZHAO QING SONG, an engineer and marketing official for a software manufacturer, had gone the full and, he now realized, barren 24 years of his life without seeing a bicycle race live until a few minutes after noon that day at the intersection of Guiping Road and Tianlin Lu in southwest Shanghai.

His immediate reaction was that he had wasted a lot of time as a spectator at such dull sports as soccer and tennis until the moment that the 104 riders in the Tour of China turned the corner in a long line of colors and whirring wheels.

"OK, it's real," Zhao shouted.

He explained that he had sometimes watched a stage of the Tour de France on television, but that this was different. "This is something we can't see on TV — this is real," he said excitedly. When the riders took the right-hand turn for the second time in their 20 laps of the 70-kilometer circuit, Zhao was in at least the sixth of the seven states of ecstasy. "Let me feel the power of the atmosphere," he exclaimed in the English he learned in school, including the Jiao Tong University in Shanghai, where he also studied engineering and injection molding.

Injection molding, which he attempted to explain, unsuccessfully — but that was not his fault — was the heart of his job at Gateway Application Technologies, a distributor of Moldflow software. He was on his lunch break, which he said typically lasts 45 minutes in China, from the factory in the Chao He New Technical Development Zone, and decided to spend it watching the third stage of the race.

Zhao was not alone. The 3.5-kilometer circuit was lined by a crowd estimated at 10,000, most of them workers and managers at the industrial park's manufacturers. Unlike Zhao, who carries the burden of management and had to return to the office halfway through, workers were given a couple of hours off to watch. They saw a good, fast race, won in a sprint by Jo Planckaert, a Belgian with the Collstrop team and the latest offshoot of the famed Planckaert family of professional riders. He was timed in one hour 32 minutes 35 seconds. Second was Arvis Piziks, a Latvian with Novell, and third was Fred Rodriguez, an American with the national team. Steve Hegg kept the yellow jersey.

"It was a good course for breakaways but there was a strong headwind, which limited the number of attempts," Hegg said. "That's why it came down to a field sprint." Most riders finished in the same time on a brisk fall day with enough of a wind to blow away the pollution that usually hovers in, over, and around Shanghai.

The spectators picked up on the sport quickly, congregating at the six corners of the course, where the action was especially intense, and at the finish line. Even the hardhats working at the many buildings going up in the vast industrial park clambered down from their bamboo scaffolding to peer over fences and applaud.

Special cheers went up for Sun Bao-hong, a member of the Kent China team, who trailed the field by a lap. His torn shorts and the huge strawberry on his right thigh showed that he had crashed on the course. Paced by a teammate, he finished to even louder cheers. There are many subtleties to bicycle racing but being a hometown boy is not among them and the crowd learned fast.

So did Mr. Kong, the bus driver, who goes by no other name. Despite his nearly 20 years' experience behind the wheel, mercifully none of them in a school bus, he learned in a day how to drive during a bicycle race.

At the start of the first stage, he did not understand that his rickety 16-seat bus was supposed to stay just far enough ahead of the riders so that they could be watched out the rear window by the reporters aboard. A few hundred meters would have been perfect but, when the riders sped off in Shenzhen, so did Mr. Kong.

Pounding on the horn despite the empty road ahead, he soon left the pack so far astern that the road behind was empty too. Cries of "Slow down" got through the language barrier all too well. Mr. Kong slowed so totally that now the riders were less than a dozen meters behind his bus and, like a torpedo, closing fast. The lead rider threw up his left arm in warning to the others and the chief official, his head visible through the top of an advance car, blew on his whistle until the veins in his neck swelled.

"Faster, go, get moving," came the cries in the bus. "Tora, tora, tora." Mr. Kong shook his head in wonder at the indecision aboard, shifted up a gear and left the pack roughly a Peoples Autonomous Region behind. Five or six further attempts at synchronization also failed.

The next day, after time to reflect on the problem, he was perfect.

Perfect? On the second stage, out of and back into Guangzhou, Mr. Kong qualified for pole position at Indianapolis. He was no greenhorn at his first bicycle race, he explained through an interpreter, but a veteran now.

From a corporate standpoint, he was even more exemplary: Mr. Kong had stowed away his black Novotel Guangzhou cap, the one with the Blue Angels pin, and donned a white and blue Kent Tour of China cap, honoring the sponsor.

Who says a bicycle race loses something in translation? Certainly not Zhao or Mr. Kong.

Writing the Book

THERE WAS NO BIBLE, as the book that charts the daily stages in a race is called, in the first Tour of China. That was because 60 percent of the course was changed in the two weeks before the race began, too late for revisions to be printed.

The prologue in Hong Kong, for example, was announced as 2.8 kilometers long and turned out to be 4.1 kilometers. The explanation was that the necessary police approval to close roads was not given until the morning before the race and the authorities chose a longer course.

These things do not usually happen in professional bicycle races, where schedules, distances and transit points are written long in advance in concrete, not rice water.

"The environment changes so radically on a dime," explained Jim Birrell, the technical director of the Tour and the man nominally in charge of selecting the route. "The Shanghai turnaround," he continued, referring to an exchange of stages in that populous city. "Just two weeks ago we agreed this is where the third stage would be and this is the fourth stage, no problem, and then they switched us. They hadn't looked at their calendar to see that there was another event, a cultural event, at the same place on the same day that we were scheduled."

Nevertheless, Birrell said, he was more than happy with the way the race was going, praising especially the work of the Chinese police. A few glitches aside, stages were starting on time, the riders had only good things to say, roads had been kept safe, and the race was moving with precision toward its finish in Beijing.

And, in spite of the switching of Shanghai's stages, the second one there attracted the largest crowds yet, some 20,000 people in the far southwestern Xing Zhang residential area. Two and three deep in some places, peering out of the windows of four- and five-story apartment houses and even standing on roofs, spectators were plentiful all along the 3-kilometer circuit, which the remaining 101 riders traversed 26 times for a total of 78 kilometers.

The easy winner in a sprint on a chilly day was again Damien Nazon in one hour 37 minutes 15 seconds, despite a crash that left him sitting on the road about halfway through. The victory allowed him to don the yellow jersey as Steve Hegg, who had been wearing it since Hong Kong, dropped to second overall, a second behind Nazon.

After the race, the Frenchman and his Castorama teammates piled aboard a bus laughing, a distinct change from their mood on the way to the morning race. The team was disappearing for financial reasons at the end of the year and most of the riders had not yet found new jobs.

"This race is too late in the season," grumbled one rider on the way out. "We should be home now, looking for a new team." On the way back, he was all smiles. Somebody joked that if Laurent Jalabert, the French star, could be acclaimed at home as "the king of Spain" after he won the Vuelta a España a few weeks before, Nazon should be dubbed "the emperor of China."

For the second successive day, the stage was held in a part of the city distant from the choked center. Nearly all eight million Shanghai residents seemed to be downtown, thronging the sidewalks and jamming the streets with bicycles and cars pretty much day and night.

"You look at all the cities we go into and how densely populated they are," Birrell said. "Can you imagine trying to close those roads downtown? You'd have to have the federales standing shoulder to shoulder, arms locked, to prevent people from getting onto the course. So we're on the outskirts of all the towns." In order, they were Hong Kong, Shenzhen, Guangzhou, Shanghai and Beijing.

If he had his druthers, Birrell would have mounted a stage along the Bund, the former European financial district at the harbor in Shanghai, and in Tiananmen Square in Beijing, both out of bounds.

"You go where the people are," he said. "If you're in New York, you go to Fifth Avenue and 59th Street," where Birrell helped design a stage for the Tour de Trump when the eponymous Donald still owned the Plaza Hotel there. "But you can imagine what it would be like if we tried to go into city centers in China in our first year," Birrell contined. "I'm glad we have the courses we have, because it allows us to see how the Chinese authorities handle it and allows them to see how we handle it. This has been a great walk-before-you-run year."

Among those Chinese authorities, the police had been zealous about crowd control, perhaps zealous to the third power. Along Xin Xi Lu — the "Lu" meaning street or route — a policeman with a bullhorn castigated a pedestrian for daring to dart across the course to a noodle shop — half an hour before the start of the fourth stage.

When roads are closed in China, they are closed: rope barriers along the course often ended by blocking access to any further sidewalk.

"I was told this is where the start is, this is where the finish is, this is how we connect the dots," Birrell said. "I had to think about the logistics: How are we going to man it, how are we going to secure the immediate start and finish areas, how are we going to build those environments?"

Nor did he have much choice in deciding which cities the Tour of China would visit. "Going to the venues that we are, that's more predicated on what the sponsor wants." Like any sponsor, Kent cigarettes preferred big markets to small ones. "The sponsor doesn't dictate but strongly suggests locations and then you go to the sports commissions and say, 'I want to bring the event here, can you find a site?"

Birrell, a Texan who was 35 years old at the time, had been laying out races since the 1984 Tour of Texas. He estimated that he had spent three months of the previous eight in Hong Kong and China preparing for the race, and he sounded wistful when he talked of his plans for the next Tour DuPont, which would start in Wilmington, Delaware, and end outside Atlanta.

"The mid-Atlantic area has it all," he said, "the flats, the shoreline, the mountains." All that territory and it was his, all his, to play with.

From Russia, with Speed

S LAVA EKIMOV did say before the Tour of China began that, although he was the only one of 104 riders to be accompanied by a wife, he had not come along to have a vacation. For her it was a vacation, he insisted. For him it was work.

He proved that in Beijing 11 days later when he won the last of six stages by 10 seconds and the overall race by a mere 2 seconds. "This is a good victory for me," he said as he rubbed a towel over his face to wipe away sweat and traces of Beijing's industrial pollution. Airborne grime never sleeps in China's cities, not even on Sundays, when workers continue to build apartment houses, office blocks, and roads.

"This victory is worth a lot to me," the Russian rider continued. Specifically it was worth $50,000 in the total pot of $200,000, which made the Kent Tour of China the world's fifth richest race after the Tours of France (the biggest, with a $2.4 million jackpot), Italy and Spain and the Tour DuPont. Ekimov's six teammates flocked around him at the finish to thump his back and shake his hand; traditionally the winner's share of a race is divided more or less evenly among teammates and support staff. Mrs. Irina Ekimov made the scene quickly too, pecking her husband on the lips. Shops in Beijing remain open late for people on vacation, and then there was the duty-free stopover in Hong Kong on the way home to Belgium.

Second by two seconds in the final stage, a 22-kilometer time trial at the Olympic Complex in north-central Beijing, far from any crowds, was Steve Hegg, who led the early part of the Tour. The man in the yellow jersey before the time trial was Daniele Nardello, an Italian with Mapei, whose future seemed immeasurable since he was just 23 years old then. Nardello, first in Paris–Bourges and second in the Tour of Lombardy in 1995, finished fourth in the race against the clock, 10 seconds behind Ekimov. The Italian started with an eight-second lead over the Russian.

Nardello gained that lead by finishing second the day before in the stage to the Great Wall while Ekimov was third, both finishing behind Alessandro Calzolari, another Italian with Mapei. Among the might-have-beens, once the Tour was over, was the 10-second bonus given Calzolari for winning; Nardello got a six-second bonus for second place, and Ekimov a four-second one for third. If the low-ranked Calzolari had let his teammate win, the extra four seconds would have given Nardello the overall victory by two seconds.

"Bah," said Patrick Lefevere, the *directeur sportif* of the Mapei team in China. "Many things could have happened. That's bicycle racing."

Ekimov was clocked in 25 minutes 28 seconds for the flat and undemanding spin at the Olympic Complex and out onto a closed six-lane highway in the midst of urban fields, gleaming new apartment houses, and dilapidated small dwellings. Overall, the Russian won in a total time of 11 hours 9 minutes 23 seconds, with Nardello those two seconds behind, and Hegg third, 11 seconds behind. The hard-luck rider of the day was Andy Bishop, an American with USPro, who fell from fifth place overall to 28th when he lost nearly three minutes on the starting stand after his rear wheel went soft and his derailleur cable snapped while the wheel was being replaced. By the time he started, Bishop was out of contention.

The final stage through urban decay contrasted remarkably with the stage the day before, 132 kilometers from the outpost of Huairou to the Great Wall. As any schoolgirl knows, especially one with an Encyclopaedia Britannica at her elbow, the Great Train Robbery, no, Great Trek, no, Great Victoria Desert, no, Great Wall of China, here it is, ran for 6,400 kilometers east to west, and parts of the fortification date to the fourth century B.C.

In 214 B.C., Shih Huang-ti, the first emperor of a united China, ordered work to begin in earnest, connecting a number of defensive walls into a single system with watchtowers. Substantially rebuilt in the 15th and 16th centuries, the wall is about 9 meters (30 feet) high, with its towers a meter higher. History does not record that, unlike the Tour of China, any other foreigners — not the traditional enemy Hsiung-nu, the nomadic tribes of the northern steppes, nor the conquering Mongol Horde under Kublai Khan — dared approach the Great Wall on bicycles. They are, in fact, forbidden atop the structure except for a Kent Tour of China photo op.

The stage's route offered a blend of the 21st century in the riders on their advanced bicycles, and perhaps the 18th century in the many peasants out working their fields with no more than hoe, shovel and rake. The only piece of farm machinery seen in more than three hours in the hills 90 kilometers north of Beijing was a mule hitched to, and walking nonstop around, a small mill to grind ears of corn into flour.

Other ears were stacked in cribs or drying on roofs in the many villages the race passed. The sole spots of green in the fields were cabbages coming to harvest just in time to be trucked into Beijing, mounded on sidewalks and sold for pickling as a winter vegetable.

The soil looked dark and rich, and Westerners based in Beijing said this was a model agricultural area compared to some provinces. For one thing, the Westerners said, these peasants grew enough not only to feed themselves but also to sell the surplus, unlike those Chinese farmers who cannot meet their own needs. Other signs of prosperity included good roads, electric power lines, and the occasional television satellite dish for an otherwise ramshackle village.

As it remained for the time trial, the weather was splendid: sunny and mild instead of the snow that fell about that time a year earlier. Above the haze of pollution, even in the hills, the sky was pure. At each brick and stone village people turned out in good numbers to see the race go by. Peasants, laying down their wooden, sledlike backpacks and their $50 Phoenix steel bicycles, seemed dumbfounded by the racers' $5,000 titanium bicycles and the accompanying fleet of about 25 cars and trucks.

The road kept climbing, steadily but rarely sharply, over three hills before it plunged over each peak into a valley. In the distance, the hills receded fainter and fainter, just as they do in scroll paintings. Now and then a faraway Great Wall observation tower could be glimpsed through leafless poplar and birch trees.

Suddenly the road came out of the hills, turned from one-and-a-half lanes into four, began mounting again, and there it was — the Great Wall, snaking overhead.

The finish was in Mutianyu — well out of the way, to limit disturbance to the major tourist thoroughfares. There were no souvenir stands, with their owners' cries of "Look, look, cheap, cheap." There were no jade Buddhas or Mao caps with a red star, no picture postcards, and no sweatshirts imprinted "I climbed the Great Wall."

Mainly there were the hills and the awesome wall. The Tour of China, in a grand part of its splendor, indeed.

3

The Race to the Sun

NEVER CELEBRATED for being politically correct, the French press unanimously predicted that the 1996 Paris–Nice race would be a piece of cake for Laurent Jalabert and his "yellow peril." That referred to Jalabert's ONCE team, which wears yellow jerseys in all races except the Tour de France, where the riders turn up in pink so as not to be confused with the overall leader.

In truth, it wasn't a hard call to pick Jalabert. He won Paris–Nice the year before and had started the season in strong and winning form. By finishing first through fifth in the Tour of Valencia in Spain, he and ONCE both showed they would be dominant. And so they were, with the Frenchman donning the leader's white jersey in Paris–Nice after his victory in the third of nine stages, increasing his advantage with a victory in the fourth stage, and then picking up bonus seconds at intermediate sprints and at finishes the rest of the way to Nice. His third place in the concluding time trial didn't hurt either. Never really threatened after the climbs, Jalabert finished 43 seconds ahead of Lance Armstrong of Motorola and 47 seconds ahead of Chris Boardman of Gan.

Jalabert's teammates rode vigilantly and well. "An impressive performance," judged Patrick Lefevere, *directeur sportif* in the race for Mapei. "ONCE was very, very strong." Besides Jalabert, his teammates Inigo Cuesta and Mariano Rojas showed why they were considered bright young hopes of Spanish racing, finishing sixth and 12th respectively. (Unhappily, Rojas was killed in a car crash in Spain that June, just before the Tour de France.) The ONCE team faced strong competition, especially from Armstrong and a powerhouse Motorola team, which also placed Laurent Madouas in ninth place, Andrea Peron in 10th, Axel Merckx in 13th and Max Sciandri in 17th. Boardman and Luc Leblanc of Polti, who was seventh, both proved that they were far back on the road from injuries the season before.

This was a revised Paris–Nice. There was no team time trial, which was dropped the year before in an attempt to prevent a blocked race, and there was no prologue either because it could not be fitted into the weeklong itinerary. And, after 26 years, the final time trial was moved from the Col d'Eze climb to flat roads along the Mediterranean, from Antibes to the Promenade des Anglais in Nice. Finally, there was no Paris in Paris–Nice. For the last few years the race had started, not in the capital, but in its dreary suburb of Fontenay sous Bois. In 1996, the start was in Châteauroux, 250 kilometers due south, in the center of France. Especially on the race's two weekends, crowds appeared to be larger and more enthusiastic than usual.

Only the weather didn't cooperate. The problem was rain, which held off at the start and abated at the finish. Wearing No. 1 because of his victory the year before, Jalabert led the pack out of Châteauroux in bright sunshine.

Stage One

RICHARD VIRENQUE wasn't intimidated, or wasn't about to show that he was intimidated, by the ONCE team. No sir. Virenque had been King of the Mountains in the last two Tours de France and regarded himself, not Jalabert, as the most popular French rider.

So, at Kilometer nine of the 175.5-kilometer flat first stage, before the 152 starters had even finished the first of two tours of the host city, Virenque went off alone on an attack. "I hoped others would join me, but they didn't," the Festina rider said. "Since I was out there, I kept going."

Thus began the mind game of the first stage.

On a sunny, clear day, with barely enough wind to ruffle the first leaves of vegetation in the adjacent pastures, Virenque quickly built a fair lead over the passive pack. When it reached 4 minutes 50 seconds at Kilometer 27, ONCE decided that enough was enough. Going to the front, Jalabert's teammates pulled the lead back to 2:30 at Kilometer 50. They let Virenque dangle there, working hard and solo, for a while.

By the feed zone at Kilometer 104, the lone racer had had enough of his training ride. He snatched his musette, began wolfing its contents and visibly slowed, expecting the pack to overtake him. But after his lead dwindled to 30 seconds and he was barely pedaling, ONCE decided to teach him a lesson for his brashness. The pack slowed too and Virenque, smiling and waving to the spectators as he drifted along, was left embarrassingly isolated in front.

Since the pack would not overtake him even at his low speed, he had two choices: stop or go. He went again, opening a lead of a minute. This was all too much for the competitive spirit of Jacky Durand, the two-time French champion who now rode for the new Agrigel–La Creuse team. He attacked, joined Virenque and rode with him, half a minute clear, until Kilometer 133. At this point,

Virenque tired of his exploit — a 122-kilometer breakaway — and slid back into the pack. Durand lasted two more kilometers.

At the finish, neither Durand nor Virenque seemed the slightest bit abashed at having wasted time and energy, nor did anyone connected with ONCE admit that the team had imposed a lesson on riders who chose to disturb the script. Put simply, the script read that the flat stage would end in a sprint. In the final 25 kilometers, Laurent Brochard of Festina and Thierry Marie of Agrigel each tried to get away but couldn't. With 20 kilometers left, Mario Cipollini's Saeco team, Wilfried Nelissen's Lotto team and Tom Steels's Mapei team led the pack, trying to set up their sprinters. Motorola was briefly up there too, although its best sprinters in Paris–Nice were Frankie Andreu and George Hincapie, neither of them a match for the top guns.

Then, coming to the line in St. Amand–Montrond after a long straightaway, there was another sprinter nobody considered a match for the Cipollinis, Nelissens and Steelses either: Frédéric Moncassin of Gan, second a week earlier in Kuurne–Brussels–Kuurne and clearly in form. Timing it just right, he finished first by parts of a wheel over Steels and Nelissen and, savoring his victory, looked equally thrilled and surprised. Cipollini, who had won five sprints in the last two Paris–Nice races but finished seventh this time, just looked surprised.

Stage Two

A NOTHER STAGE, another long solo breakaway — this time by "a regional." Not, however, the usual sort of regional, a local rider. Rather, the man cruising more than seven minutes out front was Thierry Marie, who hails from Normandy. No, Marie was not the regional but his new team was: Agrigel–La Creuse, a formation in its first year, sponsored by both a frozen-food manufacturer (Agrigel) and a French municipal *département* (La Creuse).

And guess what relation La Creuse had to the second stage? When Marie went off alone at Kilometer 10 of the 158-kilometer stage, from Dun sur Auron to Aubusson, he was just 50 kilometers up the road from La Creuse. More than an hour later, at the village of St. Pierre le Bost, in sunny and crisp weather, he crossed into the motherland, the sponsor's soil. The towns and hamlets flew by, all of them lined with spectators celebrating this exploit by somebody bearing their colors (yellow, green and a stylized blue tree, if it's not a mushroom).

Marie was a devotee of the long-distance exploit. Remember his victorious Tour breakaway across the north of France and into Le Havre a few years earlier? This time it was not to be. At Kilometer 112, on the doorstep of the finish in the carpet city of Aubusson, Marie was caught. By then he was so severely winded — this was February, the start of the season, and he was 33 years old — that he went right out the back, finishing last, nearly 14 minutes down.

As the race came through Aubusson the first time, the pack was pretty much together. There followed a 35-kilometer circuit of the city and surroundings, ending in another climb of the steep 1,100 meters to the finish. "It was a tough circuit," Andreu said, "very tight, lots of ups and downs, just like the whole stage. And that last ramp was pretty tough too."

While the uphill finish seemed ideal for Jalabert, three pure sprinters finished ahead of him. Nelissen was the clear winner, followed by Cipollini and Steels. Behind the fourth-placed Jalabert was Moncassin, who lost his leader's white jersey to Nelissen because of the time bonuses of 10, 6 and 4 seconds at the finish.

Stage Three

B EFORE THE START, Lance Armstrong had said it would be a hard day — the 170.5-kilometer third stage from Vassivière en Limousin to Chalvignac. "There are gonna be people everywhere today."

He was absolutely correct, although what he didn't say was that his Motorola team was going to make sure the stage would be hard. Armstrong left that statement till later.

Motorola attacked with 40 kilometers to go, knowing that the ramp to the finish lasted 3.8 kilometers and had an average grade of 7.5 percent and that the riders had to climb it twice, the final time after an 18.5-kilometer circuit of the village and its surroundings. "I felt the momentum had swung in our direction, because we were the ones doing the work," the Texan said. Indeed, Motorola led a long chase after Cipollini and Rojas, two early and dangerous breakaways — Cipollini because he was seeking revenge after the first two sprints, and Rojas because his third place in the Tour of Valencia showed that he was in top form. Their lead exceeded eight minutes over the up-and-down, up-and-down way to Chalvignac, filled with curves on roads that came in two widths — narrow and narrower.

Just before the feed at Kilometer 105, the two were reeled in. A few more tentative breakaways went and failed. Soon afterward, Armstrong made a key decision: "I knew there was a climb coming up and I figured we'll get our strongest guys at the front and string it out. It was perfect. There was a descent — a little dangerous and dust everywhere — and then we went straight into the climb. Perfect."

Nearly perfect. Although Motorola passed first over the top before the circuit, although the team had four men in the main chasing pack and placed three of them in the top 15 finishers, and although Armstrong himself finished second in a sprint with Boardman, the day was not perfect for Motorola. That was because, showing his strength, Jalabert climbed away from Armstrong in a two-man duel up to the finish. With about two kilometers to go, the Frenchman jumped off by seven seconds, widened it to 20 and won by 16.

Toweling himself off after the finish, Armstrong paid tribute to the winner. "No doubt about it," he said, "the best man won. Jalabert's strong. He's a sprinter, so he has a lot of acceleration." Armstrong was pleased with the team's showing, and especially with what he thought Motorola had said to ONCE. "They definitely had to work today. It wasn't a typical ONCE day — a blowaway where everybody just rolls up. Today we made 'em work for their victory."

Usually so upbeat and optimistic, Armstrong was sounding downcast and uncertain. With some of his most important races only weeks away, he could not tell how strong he was. "Top form?" he repeated. "I don't know about top form."

The problem was a bad crash in the Tour of Valencia a few weeks before. Armstrong was on a rapid descent and possibly heading for victory when he skidded on gravel and fell. He needed a week off to recover and a week was a long time to be away from his bicycle that early in the season. "I'm in good form," Armstrong admitted. "I have to see how I recovered from this crash. I certainly was heading in the right direction, but it's difficult to say now. A week off..." He let the sentence finish itself.

Afterward he remained unsatisfied. "I definitely wasn't good enough today to win a classic." The World Cup was a major objective, he continued, although he was rethinking which classics were right for him and which weren't. Of Milan–San Remo, he said, "I think that race suits my characteristics, but I always seem to have a bad day there. In the last two years I've gone in with high hopes and was disappointed. But I still think it's a good race for me.

"Flanders is another big objective," he continued. "Again a race that I think suits me, although I've always had a bad day there. I think it's time I had a good day." He was to finish far back in each in 1996 again, coming to a peak in mid-April, when he would win the Flèche Wallonne and finish second in Liège–Bastogne–Liège, his favorite spring classic.

"I did a hard winter," he reported with a certain pride. "I started earlier than usual, close to the beginning of November. But not seriously riding a bike. I did some weight training, which I'd never done before, not consistently. Lifting weights, I think that helped. I have more power. I'm stronger than other years. It was from the waist down, all leg training. I did no upper body stuff," which builds mainly useless muscle mass. "I did an awful lot of work to have a crash set me back," he concluded unhappily.

Stage Four

ARMSTRONG SAID he was feeling better, much better, both before and after the fourth stage, from Maurs la Jolie to Millau. It was a 164-kilometer race into a strong headwind that left the 139 remaining riders nearly an hour behind schedule. Nobody wanted to rush, though, since the stage finished with a climb up the Causse Noir for 7.6 kilometers with an average grade of 6.3 percent. Actually, somebody did want to rush: Frank Hoj, a Dane with Collstrop, went on an early solo breakaway that put him eleven-and-a-half minutes ahead, and then left him so weary — Thierry Marie redux — that he finished last, more than 17 minutes down.

A *causse* was the local term for any of the limestone plateaus that surround Millau, and Causse Noir translates more or less as Black Rock. And so it was Bad

Day at Black Rock for everybody except the invincible Jalabert. For the second successive day, the Frenchman pulled away from Armstrong in the final kilometer, winning by 15 seconds and widening his overall lead to 35 seconds over the American.

Armstrong attacked initially in the second half of the winding climb and he was answered by Jalabert, who then attacked himself and was answered by Armstrong. Laurent Brochard, in third place overall by 57 seconds, joined the two briefly before falling back and leaving the final two kilometers to the duel between the leaders of ONCE and Motorola.

Despite his setback on the cold and overcast climb, Armstrong later sounded pleased with his performance and that of his team. Axel Merckx, who led Armstrong and Andrea Peron into the attack on the Causse Noir, finished sixth, Madouas was seventh, and Peron 11th.

"I've got to say it again," Armstrong asserted, "the strongest man won. He's strong, he's strong, he's strong. It's no surprise, since he's No. 1 in the world. But I'm really satisfied with my effort and the way I rode. I feel much better than yesterday, which is also a good sign."

Merckx was also pleased with his own and the team's effort. A strong worker on the climb the day before, he was equally strong on stage four, leaving him in 16th place overall.

The big loser of the day was Chris Boardman. He stayed with the lead chasing group halfway up the Causse Noir, but then faded to lose 49 seconds and finish ninth. That put him more than a minute behind Jalabert, and the British leader of the Gan team had reckoned that he could not afford to trail by more than 30 seconds going into the final time trial if he hoped to win Paris–Nice.

Still, as Jalabert noted, the race was not over and a lot could still happen between Millau, stage four, and the time trial, stage eight. True, it was the ritual response to the question of whether he felt he had it all wrapped up; but, as Jalabert added in a cliche that could be chiseled into Black Rock, a race is never over until it's over. Nonetheless, with his two stage victories demonstrating his form and with his team continuing to ride strongly in support, he seemed unbeatable.

Main Man

SCHOOL WAS OUT in Maurs la Jolie so that students could watch the start of the Paris–Nice stage to Millau, talk with their favorite French riders and ask for their autographs. Richard Virenque had his clique — he is the favorite of squealing girls barely into their teens — and Luc Leblanc his, but the throng, several dozen children waiting by the gray and yellow ONCE bus, was interested only in Laurent Jalabert.

That's the way it went in all the towns and villages along the Paris–Nice route down the center of France. In Dun sur Auron a few days before, spectators spent half an hour chanting his nickname: Ja-ja, Ja-ja. In Chalvignac, after his first stage victory, he was mobbed as he left the victory podium. In Châteauroux at the start, loud applause began as Jalabert walked onto the stage with his teammates. When he was introduced, the applause turned into a standing ovation.

Granted, life is quiet in Châteauroux, almost in the dead center of the country (the monument marking that spot is a few dozen kilometers east). There were a few movies showing, there was a flea market scheduled, and there was the railroad station, which seemed to be a hangout for those with nothing else to do than watch trains rush through on their way to and from Limoges. But the big draw was Jalabert, the only one of the 152 riders to win a standing ovation.

"There are champions that everybody admires," wrote the sports newspaper *l'Equipe* of Jalabert. "They seem to come from another world, they have another dimension. And there are champions that everybody loves... because they've had their misfortunes, because they're had to earn their success, because, in addition to their talent, they resemble the rest of us."

The French understood that, and so did Jalabert, who mixed happily with all the crowds, signing any piece of paper thrust at him, chatting with one and all. He felt special warmth toward Paris–Nice, he said, since that race was the first of his major victories in 1995.

Paris–Nice was where his career really began, he said.

A year later, at age 27, and in his eighth year as a professional, he had become France's biggest sports hero. In that one year he rose from 16th place in the computerized rankings of professional riders to first, far ahead of the man then in second place, Miguel Indurain, who had won the previous five Tours de France.

Before the 1995 season, the public knew Jalabert mainly from the photograph showing him sitting on the road in Armentières with his face covered in blood after a policeman taking a photograph blocked the sprint finish of the first stage in the 1994 Tour. Jalabert went down, losing a couple of teeth and breaking his cheekbone and jaw. He needed more than three hours of surgery and then about six weeks off to recover.

Something happened to him over that next winter, something that he seemed unable to explain. He went from a sprinter, not even a top one, to a winner of a season-high 22 races, including Paris–Nice, the Milan–San Remo and Flèche Wallonne classics, and the three-week Vuelta a Espana. He finished fourth in the Tour, winning every Frenchman's heart by sweeping to easy victory on July 14, Bastille Day.

"He did it all last year," Lance Armstrong said. "He made a big bound. It's so alarming. He went from being basically one of the best field sprinters into being a guy who won the Tour of Spain."

Anybody who talked with Jalabert came away unsatisfied with his answer to what vaulted him to the top. "It's the result of several years of work," he said. "Physically and psychologically, I've grown enormously." He shied from hints that, when he was recovering from his crash, he realized that bicycle racing was more than a sport. To statements that he suddenly understood his fragility and was now overcompensating for that knowledge, he provided a wan smile. "I've learned to attack," he replied simply.

"He's very talented," said Armstrong, who had spent part of the previous winter training in Monaco with Tony Rominger, who rode five years earlier with Jalabert on the Toshiba team in France, when Jalabert was a young professional.

"Rominger says Jalabert was always good, but he was never great in training," Armstrong continued. "From what I hear, the last couple of years he's been doing some pretty mean training. And that will make all the difference in the world: If you have a big engine and you do two or three hours' training a day, you'll be good, but you'll be inconsistently good. You get that hard training done, then you'll be consistently good."

It's that simple? Jalabert paused in signing autographs the next morning to listen to the question. He shook his head pleasantly and it was impossible to decide if he agreed or not. Before the question could be put to him again, he had moved on to the next bunch of fans wanting to say hello to him, to touch him, simply to stare at him. Their cheers drowned out everything else.

Stage Five

WHO SUBTITLED Paris–Nice "the race to the sun?" What sun? There had been sun aplenty through the first three stages, but the farther south the race headed through the Midi toward its destination, the fouler the weather became. For the fifth stage, a 159-kilometer spin out of and back into Millau, an intermittent drizzle was added to the wind and heavy skies of the day before.

Neither the weather nor his loss of time in the fourth stage seemed to disturb Boardman's even temper, however. Although the Briton admitted that overall victory appeared to be impossible now, he was still hopeful of second or third place after the final time trial.

"I've only had nine days of racing," he said, "so I can't expect too much. Yesterday was disappointing. Tactically, I made no mistakes, but physically — I just can't ride the front yet." He was recovering very well, thank you, from the fractured left ankle he sustained in the rainy prologue of the previous Tour — an injury that finished his season and left him with two small screws in the heel for a good part of 1996. "But I don't know how well I'm time trialing," the Olympic pursuit champion and king of the prologues said.

"This is really the first race of the year for me," he continued, dismissing his seventh place in the Tour of the Mediterranean in February, "and the point is to see what my level is, compared to the other riders."

For the fifth stage and, really, all the ones before — he did rank fourth overall — his level was more than adequate. Boardman felt so confident about his comeback and his prospects for the year that he could afford to joke about the terrible crash that ended his season just when everybody thought it was going to begin, with a victory in the Tour prologue and the yellow jersey to hold until the mountains more than a week away.

"I had a good holiday," he said with a laugh about the months he spent first mending his body and then rebuilding his stamina and power. As he pointed out,

"I'm about 15 percent smaller in my left leg, but it doesn't seem to be a problem. It will just take time. It's more noticeable than causing me a problem."

He came in for scattered criticism after his crash for having been alone in taking risks on the slippery proglogue course. Once the downpour started, all other leading riders played it safe. Only he went all out for victory, and skidded and crashed, breaking his ankle and right wrist, on one of the last curves.

Boardman dismissed those critics: "If you get round and win the prologue under those conditions, people say, 'What a star, what bike handling, fantastic' and if you fall off, they say, 'How very rash, very irresponsible.' I don't think it was rash. I just think I made a mistake. That's my first major crash in about 1,000 race days I've had, so I'm not really complaining."

If he had it to do all over again, would he? "I'd ride in a similar vein," he answered, "and hope not to fall off." That was good for a laugh from him.

In the fifth stage, Boardman finished with the other overall leaders in a pack of 34, behind the winner by 27 seconds. The winner? Stefano Casagrande, an Italian neo-pro with MG, who made the first successful long breakaway of the race. Dominique Bozzi, a Frenchman with the new ForceSud team, aimed for that distinction too, but could not keep pace with Casagrande and was caught.

Pursuit after the Italian was retarded by a mass crash that sent Gilles Bouvard, a Frenchman with Collstrop, to the hospital along with a Lotto soigneur who was hit by a team car as he attempted to right some of his riders. Frankie Andreu, Motorola's super *domestique*, was also hurt in the crash, injuring his right knee. Although he finished the stage, he had to be taken to a hospital for stitches and would be out several weeks, missing the spring classics. "That will hurt us," said Jim Ochowicz, the team's general manager. "Frankie has good experience, one of the players we were going to count on to do a lot of the work."

Voracious for victory, Jalabert widened his lead by contesting intermediate sprints. He gained two seconds there and then won the field sprint, gaining six more. As he said, if he lost Paris–Nice, he wanted nobody to reproach him for not giving full effort. Some of the other riders, however, were beginning to question his desire to win everything in sight, and even some of the admiring French newspapers were beginning to refer to him as "the new cannibal."

Stage Six

MORE RAIN. Driving sheets of rain in the vast parking lot of one of the world's biggest, and surely one of its ugliest, shopping malls, in Vitrolles, near Marseille. After a 250-kilometer transfer by car from the fifth stage in Millau, many of the riders looked weary at the thought of a 195-kilometer stage to St. Tropez. At the sodden sign-in, a lot of them also looked as if they wished they had paid more attention in school and so had been able to land an indoor job.

Surprisingly, Boardman finished second in the sprint to the line in St. Tropez, just behind Andrei Tchmil, a Russian with Lotto, and just ahead of Max Sciandri of Motorola. The second place was worth six bonus seconds to Boardman, more

than offsetting the three seconds Jalabert picked up by winning the first intermediate spint.

"Tchmil was just a little too strong," Sciandri said. "It was a good sprint — he
can win, I can win. But he was stronger." The sprint came at the end of a stage
that saw the pack shattered by strong early winds and two second-category climbs.
On the first climb, Jalabert crashed on the descent but got back with the help of
his waiting team. Later he barely escaped another crash when a dog ran across
the road.

While the Frenchman seemed to have suffered no more than scrapes and
bruises, he really had injured his left knee, which began to pain him as the race
wound up in Nice and forced him to miss many spring races. Nobody, not even
Jalabert, realized it at the time, but his early season and his hopes of repeating
his victories in the classics had been left behind on the sixth stage.

Stage Seven

THIS WAS A STAGE that everybody feared would be a killer. Boardman had
referred to it as "a really nasty stage, another Tour of the Haut Var," with its
sharp climbs and narrow, twisting roads. But it turned out to be less than that
because of rockslides a few days earlier that blocked the way to one of the two
big climbs. Blame it on the rain.

The stage still lasted 191 kilometers, still finished in Antibes, and still left from
the tourist trap of the old port in St. Tropez. (If you're old enough to remember
Brigitte Bardot vamp her way through *And God Created Woman*, you'll remember
the port but without its souvenir shops, pizzerias, souvenir shops, cafés and
souvenir shops.) The big change was the elimination of the long second-category
climb at Tanneron, leaving the first-category climb to the gorgeous village of
Mons, with a view over the hills and valleys of Provence, as the major obstacle.

Maybe nobody remembered to tell the *peloton* that it wouldn't be such a hard
day after all. Its speed for the first hour on an overcast but neither windy nor
rainy day barely topped 27 kph, nearly at the pedestrian level. Not until the first
bonus sprint at Kilometer 31 did the pace pick up. The big boys duked it out,
going for the three-, two- and one-second primes, with Franck Vandenbroucke
of Mapei, who was in fifth place overall, crossing first, Sciandri, the designated
sprinter for Armstrong, second, and Jalabert third.

Shortly thereafter, Frédéric Pontier of Aubervilliers 93 attacked and was joined
by Ermanno Brignoli of Gewiss, Mario Scirea of Saeco, and Peter Meinert of
Telekom. In other words, an attack of no danger to any rider in the top 30 of the
remaining 112. That being so, the pack was content to let the four build a lead
that reached a maximum of just over six minutes at Kilometer 94. After the Mons
summit at Kilometer 105, Motorola tried to send Sciandri and Merckx away in
another group of four, but the pack revived and hunted them down. Later, as the
race passed hillsides of flowering mimosa bushes outside the perfume center of

Grasse and headed for the Mediterranean, Peron tried a counterattack too, but it was as vain as the first.

The four leaders were caught near the port of Antibes–Juan-les-Pins. Then such teams as Lotto, Mapei and Saeco began attempting to set up their sprinters. Nelissen was there at the front, wih Cipollini on his rear wheel and Steels not far away. Sporadic escapes were quickly quelled and, in the final kilometer, the mass sprint shaped up.

But Bruno Boscardin, an Italian with Festina, was the surprise winner, building a small lead in the straightaway and holding off the big sprinters. It was quite a coup for Boscardin, whose only previous victory in the past two seasons had been recorded in the Tour of the Haut Var. Maybe Boardman had been right — rockslide, canceled climb and all.

Stage Eight A

SCIANDRI SAID afterward that he had been feeling better every day and that he had been thinking about this 71.5-kilometer morning stage, out of and back into Nice, for a while. "Usually it's a stage for the sprinters," he said, meaning the elite, in which he did not quite rank. "So I thought maybe I could make it a stage not for them."

Mission accomplished. Sciandri spoke when he descended from the victory podium after recording Motorola's first triumph of the year. "It's good for the team to break the ice," he said. "Good for them and good for me."

He finished an easy first after a three-man breakaway with Mauro Gianetti of Polti and Jon Odriozola of Gewiss that started at Kilometer 13 in the green hills above Nice, under a weak sun — yes! sun. Quickly, their lead mounted: 30 seconds at Kilometer 24, then 55 seconds at Kilometer 26 and 1:10 at Kilometer 27. Just 15 kilometers from the finish, the lead was at 1:35 despite a strong chase led by Mapei and Gan.

With seven kilometers to go, the lead stood at 45 seconds, which dropped to 20 with two kilometers left, and 19 at the flag denoting the last kilometer. Sciandri jumped off with 200 meters to go and easily held off Odriozola, with Gianetti third, and the pack, led by Steels, seven seconds back.

Stage Eight B

JALABERT HAD NEVER won a time trial as a professional, and he did not set a first here. Boardman had rarely lost a time trial, pro or amateur, and he did not lose this one. So what was new?

The surprise was that Armstrong finished second — 24 seconds behind Boardman and 5 ahead of Jalabert — and retained his second place overall by 4 seconds. It was arguably the Texan's strongest race in a flat time trial in his four seasons as a professional. Armstrong knew he had to go all out to hold off

Boardman, and he did, completing his effort with an out-of-the-saddle sprint over the last 50 meters.

The winter work with weights for his legs showed in the 19.9- kilometer course from Antibes to Nice, alongside the curling waves of the Mediterranean. A big crowd watched in overcast and slightly windy weather, giving Armstrong a round of applause for his fine time.

But he did not look happy as he stood on the three-man victory podium. His third second-place stage finish of the week, combined with his second place overall, probably nettled him. He was, after all, eager for victory and had often said that second place was the worst of all places.

Boardman was somewhat downcast too, because he did want to finish second. "I really hoped to overtake Lance," he said. "Other than that disappointment, I'm very happy with my ride."

Well he should have been. At 12:40, the fastest man by far at the intermediate point, he poured on the coal thereafter to triumph convincingly and show everybody that he had fully recovered from the Tour injury.

The big loser was Luc Leblanc, who finished a weak 24th and dropped from third place overall to seventh. Franck Vandenbroucke, fifth in the time trial, moved up to fourth and Laurent Brochard, fourth in the time trial, moved up to fifth. Something for nearly everybody, including that feeble glow in the sky above the Race to the Sun.

Family Ties

WHO WAS IT who first noticed "How sharper than a serpent's tooth it is to have a thankless child"? Not Jean-Jacques Vandenbroucke, a mechanic with the Lotto team. Not Jean-Luc Vandenbroucke, the team's *directeur sportif*.

No, it was King Lear, not the Brothers Vandenbroucke. They said it later.

In 1995, Franck Vandenbroucke, the bright young hope of Belgian racing, quit their team. He left the father, Jean-Jacques, and uncle, Jean-Luc, who took him to races as a child and gave him his first bicycle and his first lessons in the sport, who nurtured him through the amateur ranks and signed him to his first professional contract and said the Lotto team would be structured around him.

In 1995, they called him thankless when he went to court in Belgium to break his contract with Lotto and, at age 20, move to the Mapei team in Italy. "Thankless" was one of their gentler words in 1995.

"Our relations are good now," Franck Vandenbroucke said a year later. "They weren't so great with Jean-Luc but now they're OK. Now there are no problems." He looked over his shoulder as if afraid of being overheard and contradicted.

"It was impossible for me to work for my family," he continued during Paris–Nice, where he finished fourth. Winner of the esteemed Paris–Brussels race the season before, he had started the new year with a victory in the Tour of the Mediterranean. He climbed and time-trialed strongly, he sprinted, he won long, flat races like Paris–Brussels, he was only 20 — no wonder Jean-Luc Vanden-broucke wanted to keep him with Lotto.

Franck Vandenbroucke was straightforward in explaining his move to Mapei. "I would have signed originally with another team, but the family asked me please to go with Lotto, and it was only after I did that I realized it wasn't good for me," he said. "It was impossible to take orders from somebody in the family. I couldn't stand it."

"One thing is sure: He has a big talent," said Patrick Lefevere, the *directeur sportif* for Mapei in Paris–Nice. "He's very, very strong. The only thing he doesn't have is a big physical frame, but he's still young and has to be a bit patient. He's very impatient."

Lotto, Lefevere thought, would have been the wrong team for the young Vandenbroucke. "Not international enough. I don't think he can find a team better for him than ours. We have the money, we have a big organization, we have everything. We have 30 riders, so we can give a young rider time to race when he wants to and then time to get some rest."

Over at the Lotto car, Jean-Luc Vandenbroucke, himself a fine rider a decade before, agreed with Lefevere. "He's a super rider, a pure talent," he said of his nephew. "Considering his age, if he finishes in the first five here, that will promise a lot for his future. If he handles it right, he can have a great career."

That was the objective analysis. The subjective one was more solemn.

"We don't talk much and it's not the same," he said. "I was very hurt and the whole thing left me feeling pretty bad. That's life. He chose his life, I chose mine. We carry the same name and that's about it."

A few minutes later, Franck Vandenbroucke rode by the Lotto car on his way back from the sign-in for the stage. Jean-Luc Vandenbroucke put up a hand. His nephew stopped.

They had a long conversation, the Mapei rider and the Lotto coach. From a distance they looked almost intimate.

Paying a Debt of Honor

THE TRAVELER on the French road D-105, one lane each way in the Cantal region of the southwest, would almost certainly be heading toward some destination other than Chalvignac. Pleaux, perhaps, or Mauriac, which are at least towns, or Aurillac, which is, stretching it a bit, a small city.

Chalvignac is a village. Population 600. A post office, a couple of cafés, a few dozen houses surrounded by pastures and planted fields that were just then turning green. D-105 climbs a hill to Chalvignac, offers a pleasant view of the Dordogne River, bends broadly through town, and then heads off to the horizon, to Pleaux, perhaps, or Mauriac.

Not many people stop in Chalvignac. In 1995 the Paris–Nice bicycle race was supposed to finish a daily stage there and, to hear the residents talk, it was going to be one of the bigger events in the village's history.

The weather turned to snow that day in 1995, however, and the wind was sharp and strong, blowing the snow across D-105 and blocking it. After fighting the wind and snow for a while, and falling far behind the race schedule, the riders refused to go further. Rarely is a bicycle race canceled because of a storm, but this one was. Paris–Nice moved off in cars and buses to wherever the teams were staying that night. The next day the race resumed far from Chalvignac.

The village was installed early in the 1996 itinerary. "A debt of honor," said Josette Leulliot, who has directed Paris–Nice since 1982, succeeding her father, Jean Leulliot, who started the race in 1933. "Yes, exactly," she continued, "a debt of honor that we owe to Chalvignac."

The weather was fine in 1996, and the race proceeded there without incident. On the long climb up the hill, Laurent Jalabert attacked early and gained a 16-second victory, taking the overall leader's white jersey. Afterward he stood on a shoulder of D-105, signing autographs and chatting with people from the village, a millionaire wearing short pants on his visit to Chalvignac.

The village turned the day into a holiday, complete with fatted calf. It was turning on a spit over a fire in the main square. "All the animals that we serve come from our farm," a sign announced. For 65 francs ($13), lunch comprised cold cuts, a slice of roast beef, the local whipped potatoes called *aligot*, and finally an assortment of cheese. For 50 francs, no cold cuts.

Other stands sold sandwiches — paté, cheese or sausage — and waffles and crêpes. For drinks, this being France, wine was cheaper at 7 francs than water (8 francs).

The villagers had set up a big tent in the square and, after the race, they gathered there to listen to a few speeches of welcome to the race, to drink a glass or three of *pastis* and to nibble at pieces of the local cheeses — *cantal* and roquefort.

A band was going to play and each table in the tent held copies of songs for a singalong. The top sheet was titled "To the Country Market," a regional waltz with words by René Labourel and music by Altero Betti.

Roughly translated, the verse runs: "In this country is born / The most beautiful market / On the bank of the Dordogne / Where every Saturday night / Chalvignac receives / All the kings of folklore." In part, the refrain: "Chalvignac, I love you / With your great market / Each weekend / I come to enjoy / The good products of the Auvergne." In all, there were three verses, each one followed by the refrain.

The singing had not yet started when it was time for the Paris–Nice troupe to head for that night's hotels, far from Chalvignac, but no doubt the celebration went on into the night.

As they say in this sport, it is not enough to bring people to the race. The race must also go to the people.

4
Hell of the North?

BICYCLE RACING, the maxim goes, is an individual sport practiced by teams. But not in the centennial edition of the lordly Paris–Roubaix classic over the cobblestones in the north of France. Collective interests were all that mattered there.

Showing why it started the 1996 season ranked as the No. 1 professional team, the Mapei-GB team captured the first three places in the 263.5-kilometer race, and four of the first five. Like many of the 27 teams in Paris–Roubaix, Mapei was allowed eight starters.

"It's a terrific victory but it was a team effort," said the winner, Johan Museeuw, a Belgian, in a major understatement. His victory was predetermined by team needs and guaranteed by team discipline from the moment that Museeuw and two teammates, Gianluca Bortolami and Andrea Tafi, both Italians, broke away from a group of 21 leading riders with 85 kilometers to go.

Those were three big motors. Museeuw was the defending champion in the World Cup series of classics, and ranked fifth in those standings before the start of Paris–Roubaix. Bortolami and Tafi had been racing strongly all spring. But the Mapei team, which is based in Italy, needed to favor Museeuw in his defense of the World Cup title. So, when he had a flat shortly after the breakaway, his teammates slowed and waited for him. When he had another flat with less than 10 kilometers to the finish, they slowed and waited again.

Finally, when they swung off the last of 22 sections of bone-shaking cobblestones and entered the sunny velodrome at Roubaix, Bortolami and Tafi obediently if unhappily lined up behind Museeuw as the three glided around the track. With a few hundred meters to go, Tafi raised both his arms in triumph, and then Bortolami did the same.

Museeuw, who had already won nearly every other major classic but not Paris–Roubaix, waited until the last moment before joining them in the salute.

Then he headed for the podium and collected the traditional cobblestone given to the winner. This time, though, to mark the centennial of Paris–Roubaix, the block of granite was gold-plated. (Despite the 100th anniversary, this was the 94th edition of the endurance contest, which was interrupted by both world wars.)

With the victory, Museeuw moved back atop the World Cup standings, where he remained at the end of the season. The Belgian finished in 6 hours 3 minutes, with Bortolami and Tafi in the same time, a speedy average of 43 kilometers an hour. Stefano Zanini, an Italian with Gewiss, was fourth and Franco Ballerini, another Italian with Mapei, fifth, both 2:43 late.

Thereafter it was nearly three more minutes to the next small bunch of finishers among the 184 men who started. Only 56 made finally made it. Happily, there was none of the rain that often makes the cobblestones so slippery and treacherous that Paris–Roubaix is nicknamed "The Hell of the North." The weather was so sunny and balmy, in fact, that the race might have been called "The Hell of the Riviera."

If Museeuw was a beneficiary of team needs, Ballerini, in fifth place, was a victim of them. He was the defending champion in Paris–Roubaix, in which he had often had terrible luck. In 1993, for example, he lost a photo finish to Gilbert Duclos-Lassalle for victory and vowed never to return. He did, though, and in 1994 finished third despite five flats and three crashes. He won easily in 1995 and his luck seemed to have changed.

But no. Just as his three teammates attacked in the centennial edition and started their triumphant roll toward Roubaix, Ballerini had another flat. When he tried to reach them after repairs, he again had a flat. By then, Ballerini had been joined by rivals and had no choice but to drop his efforts and not help opponents against his teammates up ahead. A third flat settled his hash definitively.

Later, with the caked dust of the road washed off, Ballerini, Bortolami and Tafi must have had an interesting conversation about what might have been. Museeuw had already left by then for his home, not far across the border in Belgium.

Worker Bee

GEORGE HINCAPIE had just finished Paris–Roubaix, which was more than 130 of the 183 other starters could say, but he was obviously unhappy. The thick coating of dust on his face could not hide his disappointment.

"I didn't have it in my legs when I needed to," said Hincapie, a bright young hope of American racing. "No mechanical problems, nothing went wrong with my equipment." He leaned his bicycle against his Motorola team car and started to head for the showers at the finish of the race, which is studded with 22 strips of cobblestones that total 50 kilometers.

"The power just wasn't there," he said mournfully. Twenty-ninth in 1996, 21st in Paris–Roubaix the year before, 31st in 1994 — Hincapie was showing consistency at least. But, as the native New Yorker neared his 23rd birthday, he was seeking more than consistency among those riders who finish five or seven minutes behind the winner.

Especially in Paris–Roubaix. "It's something I really get motivated for," Hincapie said before the start in Compiègne, north of Paris, where the endurance race begins. "Now that I've done Paris–Roubaix a few years, I know that even if you have good legs, you need good luck too. I know that I'm feeling well and I have to hope that everything goes right, that I don't have any problems."

For a while, everything went right. When the decisive attack by 21 riders began two-thirds of the way into the race, Hincapie was among the group. He could not hold his place, however, at the next attack and fell behind as the lead group splintered.

That was frustrating but not unexpected. "I'm not yet as strong as Museeuw, Ballerini or guys like that," he said beforehand, referring to Johan Museeuw, who won the race, and Franco Ballerini, the defending champion, who finished fifth this time. "Even when you're in the first group with 40 or 50 kilometers to go, that's still a long way. Last year I was in the first group" near the end of the cobblestones when the victorious attack began "and I couldn't hold the wheel. My legs were empty."

Despite his record as a dominant amateur rider in the United States from 1991 through 1993, Hincapie had to work hard to build the strength he needed as a professional in Europe. Six feet three inches tall, he weighed only 185 pounds, including the goatee he sometimes sported.

He recorded two victories in 1995, after three in 1994 and a second-place finish in the Tour of Luxembourg. For his age, his prospects seemed bright and his dedication was unquestioned. "I did a lot of work over the winter, weight training, more serious, more intense training," he said. "I trained hard the winter before that too, but when I came over to Europe, I got sick early and that's hard to bounce back from."

Moving from his family home in Farmingdale, Long Island, to Charlotte, North Carolina, three years earlier, he now took advantage of the milder winter weather to do more mountain biking. "For sure it helps in a race like Paris–Roubaix," he said. "A lot of hard riding on single-track trails, muddy, lots of tight turns and riders falling." Although he was talking about mountain biking, he might have been describing Paris–Roubaix in the rain.

This race was his first major objective of the season. Next came the Tour DuPont in May in the United States, and then the five races to select the five-man U.S. team for the road race at the Olympic Games in Atlanta.

"The trials will be hard because when you're on Motorola, a lot of American teams are riding against you," he said. "The good thing is that they're hard courses so it should be just the strong riders up front." He meant, among others, himself. He did make the Olympic team and, riding solely in support of Lance Armstrong, finished 76th.

Hincapie started racing at age 11, following the example of his father, who worked in the mail department of John F. Kennedy International Airport and who raced himself for 20 years in Queens, Manhattan and Nassau County, Hincapie said. "He still goes out once in a while and so does my brother Richard, but he's working for a computer company now, so can only train two hours a day and race just on weekends for the Mengoni team."

As a youth, Hincapie rode on the same metropolitan New York circuit for the Mengoni team, sponsored by Fred Mengoni, the longtime friend and patron of Greg LeMond. He also raced for the Toga team and for the Somec-Stuyvesant bicycle shop. "Lots of races in Central Park," he remembered.

In most of his races in Europe, he rode mainly as a *domestique*, a worker bee for Motorola's two strongest men, Armstrong and Max Sciandri. "It depends what race I'm doing. In Paris–Nice, I knew I was just there to help. In the Tour of Flanders, I had to do a little work for the team.

"In one section, Lance got into a bad position — one group got away and I had to close that gap. It took me a while to recover from that. I was in the red zone for a while. But that's something you've got to do, and that's something I want to do, because Lance had a chance to win the race. When you've got someone like Lance or Max on the team, you've got to give them everything. I know that's my job. They're two of the best in the world. But in Paris–Roubaix, I consider myself one of the guys who should be up there. Maybe also in some stages of the DuPont, maybe I'll be up there and the other guys will help me out. I feel strong. I'm happy with the way I've felt up to now."

Hung Up in Picardy

VINCENT LAVENU smiled at one and all, shook any hand in reach, turned appropriately solemn to discuss his team's prospects in Paris–Roubaix.

Paris–Roubaix! Definitely the big time. The Hell of the North. The centennial edition of Paris–Roubaix, with four hours of coverage on European television. This was more like it for Lavenu, the *directeur sportif* of Petit Casino–C'est Votre Equipe. Nodding happily, he turned realistic.

"What chance do we have against some of these big teams?" he asked. "Big cylinders, some of them. We're small cylinders."

He knew what he was talking about: The only member of his six-man team who would finish was Jaan Kirsipuu, an Estonian, in 16th place. Lavenu is no fool but, even in realistic moments, he is enthusiastic.

"It's beginning to happen for us," he said. "Two second places, you noticed that? Two second places. For us, the season really begins now."

The two second places, scored early in April, were in the distinctly minor Circuit de la Sarthe stage race. Lavenu's team was usually found in minor races, not in such crown jewels of the World Cup as Paris–Roubaix.

When the World Cup competition began in March with Milan–San Remo in Italy for the 22 first-division teams, his second-division team was riding in

Cholet–Pays du Loire deep in France. When the big boys were riding the Tour of Flanders in Belgium, his team was at the Grand Prix de Rennes in deeper France. The next weekend, when the first division would ride Liège–Bastogne–Liège, the second division would be in such smalltime races as A Travers le Morbihan and the Tour de la Côte Picarde in deepest France.

Morbihan! Picardy! Backwaters. Lavenu winces. His heart yearned for Liège–Bastogne–Liège, the big time.

The problem, of course, was money. With an annual budget of 6.5 million francs ($1.5 million), he could not compete for star riders with the first-division teams: Banesto spent more than $6 million a year, Gewiss ditto, Mapei and ONCE, don't ask. Gan, then the sole first-division team in France, had a budget of nearly $5 million. In contrast, the five French second-division teams ranged from a bit above $1 million (Mutuelle de Seine et Marne) to not quite $2 million (Agrigel–La Creuse).

As a small team with a small budget, Petit Casino–C'est Votre Equipe was eligible only for the World Cup races in its own country. Of the 11 classics, that meant just Paris–Roubaix in the spring and Paris–Tours in the fall. In between, it was the small time: Cholet, Rennes, the Tour of Armorique, places virtually unknown to first-division teams. Picardy!

Lavenu, then 40, was daunted neither by the races nor by his team's lackluster performance. He would not react the way Willy Teirlinck, the *directeur sportif* of Collstrop, a minor team in Belgium, did that month when his riders showed no spark in a stage race: Teirlinck recalled his staff from the feed zone and made his riders finish two stages in the cold rain without food, without fuel.

Collstrop and Petit Casino had the same number of victories so far that season — none — but it was not Lavenu's way to be harsh. He remembered how it felt to be a minor rider trying to stay with those with stronger legs and more talent, the big cylinders. Instead of anger, he offered understanding.

"It's a young team with a lot of spirit," Lavenu had said hopefully, earlier in the season. The only Petit Casino rider with a name was Armand De Las Cuevas, whose talent was often obscured by his attitude. The year before, the Castorama team that he led suspended him without public explanation from mid-July through the end of the season in November. "He's a rider of high quality, a little different, but a leader," Lavenu said. "His signing will give us a little more cachet."

Cachet was what Lavenu desperately needed. In his fifth year as a *directeur sportif*, his goal was, as always, an invitation to the Tour de France. He usually got it, and his undermanned team always rode dismally. But it was the big time, and Lavenu bubbled the entire three weeks.

"The Tour de France is the main goal of all French teams," he said. "I think De Las Cuevas is an extra trump." The Tour's organizers had already issued invitations, all of which were accepted, to the top 18 teams in the computer rankings. Petit Casino ranked 23rd. Four wildcards would be awarded in June and Lavenu was optimistic.

"We'll go to the Tour de France," he began confidently, "if we deserve to." His voice dropped away on the last few words.

Petit Casino was not alone in its despair. These were hard time for French teams, which could not find sponsors to provide the millions needed to compete for the best riders. Blame it on the economy, which remained torpid with more than three million people unemployed. Growth projections for the year had just been revised sharply downward, from 2.8 percent to 1.3 percent, barely a pulse.

So Lavenu had to make do with smaller sponsors. Starting in 1992, it was Chazal, a regional merchandiser of cold cuts. In 1996 it was Petit Casino, a chain of coffee shops in supermarkets, that was contributing more than half his team's budget.

"Listen," he said, "the name is not just Petit Casino. The 'C'est Votre Equipe' is very important." It means "It's Your Team" and literally it is; anybody out there wanting to become a sponsor, send a contribution. 'C'est Votre Equipe' is a concept to let the public become part of the team, to have a say for a minimum of 150 francs," he explained.

"Already we have 1,200 supporters, even people in Belgium, in Luxembourg. In France our supporters range from people on welfare to the heads of companies. They send us their checks, we send them information, a team book, and we'll do that all year long. A drawing will be held to see who follows a race with us, rides in the team car. And all year long, information about the team."

Personal checks accepted, no credit cards. The address: France Cyclisme Promotion, 9 rue du Genevois, 73000 Chambéry le Haut, France. From his heart, Vincent Lavenu said thanks and looked forward to seeing you at the team's next race, A Travers le Morbihan. Morbihan! Picardy!

5
In America

PEERING AROUND the hotel lobby in Wilmington, Delaware, Tony Rominger announced that he really liked the United States, watery coffee and all. "My wife, she would like when I retire that we should live in the States, California maybe," he said. Rominger thought he would prefer the East Coast because it was three or four hours closer to Europe by air, more convenient for trips back to his native Switzerland.

Then the world's No. 2 rider, behind Laurent Jalabert, Rominger was getting a chance to look over real estate for the next week and a half while he competed in the 1996 Tour DuPont as the leader of the Mapei–GB team from Italy. It was one of 16 teams of 7 riders each that started the 1,225-mile DuPont in Wilmington, heading for the outskirts of Atlanta.

This was not his first trip to the United States, Rominger explained. "Twice in Colorado, three times in San Diego, always for a month of training" in the winter, he said. "Nice scenery, nice weather, nice people."

He liked to travel. Then 35 years old, he planned to retire either at the end of that season or the next one and go touring. "Maybe I'll take some long vacations, half a year, to see the world, to see its people, its cultures. Now we're traveling the whole world but we don't see anything. We see the inside of hotels, we see the airports, that's all."

Retirement, he continued, would depend on motivation, not on success.

"It depends if I still love my sport. If I'm still motivated — the training, the life of a cyclist — I will do one year more. But if I see it's getting too hard to stay motivated, I will stop at the end of this year. At most, only one year more. That's for sure.

"It will depend on how I'm going. If I'm training a lot, giving it my best, and I'm not able to stay with the strongest riders, I'll stop. But if I do one more year, it will not be as the team leader. I'd like to do the Tour de Suisse next year, and try to win it — not what I've ever done — and then go to the Tour de France as an *équipier* for Abraham Olano. They gave me so much, the Spanish guys, I would like to give them back something.

"You know, it's a fantastic sport but sometimes you're not so happy. You think, 'I have to train again today?' When I say 'I want to stop now,' I'll be happy."

Rominger was not riding the DuPont — in which he eventually finished third — with much expectation of victory, he admitted. For one thing, he was behind in his condition because of a two-week bout with bronchitis in March, which left him trailing the field in most of his spring races in Spain. For another, his season would not really begin before the start of the Tour de France late in June.

"My goal is to go strong from the start of the Tour de France and continue strong up to the end of the season, including the world road championship" in Lugano, Switzerland, in October.

He intended to ride in the Olympic Games too. "Not in the road race," he said, "only the time trial. But I will ride the pursuit on the track if the Tour de France goes bad for me." The pursuit was scheduled just three days after the Tour ended and most other riders planned to skip it because of the six-hour time difference with their European eating and sleeping habits and the difficulty in adjusting quickly.

Not Rominger, who admitted that he could be single-minded. "If I don't have the shape in the Tour de France," he said, "I will drop out and do the pursuit."

When he does retire, Rominger will be able to look back on a splendid career. He won the Vuelta a España from 1992 through 1994 and the Giro d'Italia in 1995. He set the record for the hour's ride against the clock at 55.2 kilometers in 1994, which stood until Chris Boardman exceeded it at 56.3 kilometers late in 1996.

That left only the Tour de France among the big stage races still to be won by Rominger. The closest he came was second place in 1993. And that was why he was riding for the first time in the DuPont, which ranked itself, somewhat grandly, as the world's fourth-most-important race.

"The Tour de France," Rominger said, "this year I'll be approaching it differently. This year it's the first big goal of the year for the first time. Before, I did the Vuelta first and I always won it easily. Last year, I did the Giro first and I won by seven minutes. So I reached my objectives and I went a little bit down psychologically. I knew I had done my work for the sponsor. If I could do something more, OK, but the most important thing, it was done.

"I think that's not the best preparation for the Tour de France. You have to come there with big pressure from the team, from yourself, that you have to do really well in the Tour.

"That's the big difference this year: to come to the Tour de France with nothing big done before. You have to show something. If not, it will be a bad year."

Whose training idea was this? "Mine," he said proudly. "I looked last fall at the last four years and I said I have to change something. You can't always do the same. You need new goals, new motivations.

"If I win the Tour de France, it would be great. If I don't win, it's not the end of the world. I will go to the Tour de France to do my best. If I do a good job, I will be satisfied. I would like to win it surely, but I've arrived at the point..." He paused to consider his career. "I was the No. 1 racer in the world, I reached more than I expected when I started my career. Ten years ago nobody would have said that I could one day win the Giro, win the Vuelta. They would have said, 'He's a great rider but only for 10 days.'

"It's the age," Rominger said firmly. "You have to learn how to build up your muscles, you have to learn how to race, you learn how to recover faster."

He noted that he had not started racing seriously until he was at the relatively late age of 22 and that he had suffered for years from pollen troubles in the summer, which hampered him in the Tour. These days, he said, the pollen troubles were much diminished.

A bigger problem than clogged sinuses was, of course, Miguel Indurain. Rominger shook his head in mock dismay at the mention of the Spaniard's name.

"The last four years in the spring I always beat him, and then comes the Tour de France and he's always the strongest guy in the pack." The Swiss saw no reason for that to end in 1996, but beyond that he was wary.

"A new generation is coming," Rominger said. "They haven't done it yet but I think this is the last Tour de France for Indurain. He can win this year again, but next year I don't think so."

He ran off the names of the main contenders, starting with Evgeni Berzin of the Gewiss team: "Berzin has the most class but he's a Russian. That means if he has a big contract, I'm not sure he will win big races. When he has to compete for a new contract, he will be there. Then Jalabert, I think he can win the Tour de France. Zülle, Riis, they will be there." The young Italians who had looked so good in the spring classics? "In two or three years that's possible, but not at the moment.

"Riders like me and Indurain, we've been dominating the last six, seven years. That's a long time for a career; in modern cycling, that's a long time.

"I don't understand this: Indurain's always so strong in the Tour de France, never bad luck, never, nothing. He never gets sick, never has a flat. The last two years I wasn't so good, but three years ago I was there for winning and I had such bad luck — penalties, flats, I had to start early in the time trial and it rained early, but not when Indurain started. That was really bad luck.

"I was so strong that year. I won the best climber, I won three mountain stages, I had such good results." And, by 4 minutes 59 seconds, finished second to Indurain.

A Happy Man

BICYCLE RACING was fun again, Andy Hampsten said, and life was good. He had become a father for the first time that winter, he felt useful to his team after a dry spell in Europe, and he had rediscovered his zest. And, he said, it was a holiday racing again in America, where Hampsten was competing in the Tour DuPont for the first time since 1990.

"It's always been fun racing in the United States," he explained. "Racing is so much more serious in Europe. The atmosphere of a race doesn't have to be so grim."

Then aged 34 with an impressive record of victories, two fourth places in the Tour de France and years of service as a team leader, Hampsten sounded ready for a mellow period. He was still looking for triumphs but overall he had reached that point where less is more.

"I'm happy with my career," he judged. "Obviously there are all kinds of races I wish I'd won — seconds and fourth places that I wish had been victories, a lot of small races where I realized I had really good form, none of them were big — I can look back now and think, 'Boy, I should've, I had the form, I should've put those fourths and fifths together into a victory.'

"But they're not even regrets — they're lessons, and I'm grateful for them.

"On paper, my career could have been better. I never won the Tour de France, never even got on the podium. But I also think I've raced to the best of my ability. It's not as if I can say 'I would've been on the podium if...' No. In short, I think I've done the best with my ability.

"I've always felt my career happened at the right time, just when cycling was getting started in the U.S. thanks to Greg LeMond. So I'm real happy. I'm also happy I'm concluding my career. I know I'm no longer at the top, that I can't call all the shots and be in the top five in any race I want to. If things don't go well, this will be my last year. If they do go well, one more year, two more years.

"I'm on a really nice team," he said. "I don't think I'd be racing any more if I wasn't on this team," referring to U.S. Postal Service, a new team with big ambitions but a moderate program. "The team is compatible. Like there are two sprinters and they totally get along, no rivalry. Not with many teams would that happen. They appreciate me. It's not that they can't function without me, but I'm able to give my experience to the team. So it's enjoyable being in races with them. That's more important now to me than being on a big team and going to the best races and being right in the focus. I'd just rather not deal with big international pressures."

Hampsten looked, sounded, and acted relaxed, which had not always been the case the last few years when he was coping with the pressure of being a star American rider, the longtime leader of 7-Eleven and Motorola before he became a support rider for Miguel Indurain in his quest for a fifth victory in the Tour de France the year before.

Indurain had notched that victory, but Hampsten had not been there to help. A rider who had won the Giro d'Italia, two Tours of Switzerland and the

1 (top left) Andrei Tchmil and Franco Ballerini in the Het Volk (James Startt photo)

2 (top right) Miguel Indurain struggling up a climb (Beth Schneider photo)

3 (below) Bjarne Riis leading Laurent Jalabert on a climb (James Startt photo)

4 (top left) The Great Wall looms over a finish in the Tour of China (James Startt photo)

5 (top right) Lance Armstrong, proud Texan, in the Tour DuPont (Beth Schneider photo)

6 (below) The Paris–Nice peloton heading south, toward the sun (James Startt photo)

7 (top left) Armstrong climbing Beech Mountain in the DuPont (James Startt photo)
8 (top right) Andy Hampsten in U.S. Postal colors (Beth Schneider photo)
9 (below) Frankie Andreu, Motorola strongman (James Startt photo)

10 (top left) Patrick Lefevere explains Mapei team strategy (James Startt photo)

11 (top right) Chris Boardman climbing (James Startt photo)

12 (below) Eddy Merckx pacing his son Axel on a motorcycle (James Startt photo)

13 (top left) Frédéric Moncassin, winner of two Tour stages (James Startt photo)
14 (top right) Mario Cipollini, Il Magnifico (James Startt photo)
15 (below) Erik Zabel beats Cipollini in a Tour sprint (Beth Schneider photo)

16 (top left) Bjarne Riis, winning the Tour stage into Sestrière (Beth Schneider photo)

17 (top right) Evgeni Berzin of Gewiss (James Startt photo)

18 (below) Riis raising Indurain's arm in Pamplona (Beth Schneider photo)

19 (top left) Daisuke Imanaka of Polti (Beth Schneider photo)

20 (top right) Jan Ullrich of Telekom (Beth Schneider photo)

21 (below) Tony Rominger, his knee bandaged, at Hautacam (Beth Schneider photo)

22 (top left) Eros Poli on a long and unsuccessful breakaway (James Startt photo)

23 (top right) Abraham Olano in his world champion jersey (James Startt photo)

24 (below) Laurent Jalabert struggling in the Alps (Beth Schneider photo)

formidable Alpe d'Huez climb in the Tour de France, Hampsten was left off the nine-man Banesto team for the Tour. He spent the summer at his home in Tuscany, Italy.

"It was between me and a couple of other guys for the last position, and the other guys were winning mountainous races," he explained. "They wanted my experience, I was riding well, I didn't have any problem but I wasn't super.

"That was a disappointment for me. The whole experience of Banesto was very good, to be with the best team, but I needed more stimulation to do better racing. I did the Giro for them, and I didn't want to do the Giro and I didn't enjoy it. It's no longer a pleasure just doing the Giro. I was a little bit over my head — it's gotten a lot harder. There used to be 10 or 20 guys racing hard, now it's 50 or 60. I didn't have the motivation. Why was I doing the Giro? Because the team wanted me to. And that doesn't interest me any more: The team sent me, so I have to do a good job."

Stimulation has always been important to him. The son of college teachers in North Dakota, he was that rare rider who will wander a town after a race, looking at the architecture, tasting the local foods, visiting the museums. Hampsten always had books with him during a race. He enjoyed learning languages and studied the Spanish guitar during his time with Banesto.

Another interest was his home in Tuscany, which he and his wife, Linda, had been remodeling from an old farm house for the last few years. "It's pretty much finished, but now that we have the baby, we don't care," he said. Their daughter is named Emma.

"We're going to stay on there. We also have a little house in Colorado that we rent out, so we always have that for an option, maybe come back for a summer, maybe for a year." He knew what he would do when he retired: "I'll be a hobby farmer. We have a little bit of land and that can keep me very busy. For a year or two, to step away from cycling, I could be happy with that."

Why not? He had been at it for quite a while. At 34, he was a decade removed from his professional debut with the powerhouse La Vie Claire team based in France and headed by Bernard Hinault and Greg LeMond. While they dueled for victory in the 1986 Tour — LeMond finally first, Hinault second — Hampsten finished fourth and won the white jersey of the best young rider. He credited Hinault, then in the last season of his distinguished career, with having taught him how to adjust to the professional's life.

"He would talk to me even though I couldn't communicate that well. He would show us in the race, if people had their eyes open, how he wanted help, instead of having a team meeting and saying, 'You guys have to do this and that.'

"I didn't know him before '86 but he was probably more generous in the transfer of his knowledge then than at any other time. A guy like Niki Ruttimann," a Swiss rider with Vie Claire, "who had dedicated himself to helping Hinault, when Niki had a chance to win a race like Midi Pyrenees, Hinault would just kill himself to help him win.

"Same for me in the Tour of Switzerland. I was the new guy on the team and the first stage, for example, I was a neo-pro and wearing the yellow jersey and it was raining, but I wanted to show off my yellow jersey and I didn't wear a rain jacket all day and he could see I was in big trouble at the end and he found me and 'How you doing, Andy?' 'Not too good.' And he said stick with me and he'd slide back and bring me up.

"I probably would've blown up. He was dedicated to me. And I learned more in a few days like that than from some *directeur* blowing smoke in my face and 'Do this, do that.' "

Now Hampsten was the veteran and, as he said, "If I can pass a little bit on to these guys, you can say it's a little duty of mine. But not heavy-handedly. I know better than to tell these guys who have a lot of talent, 'You have to do this,' because they have to use their talent."

The team was planning to ride in June in the Tour of Switzerland, its major European race that season. It was also Hampsten's major race. His voice grew dreamy as he talked about the possibility of winning there a decade after his triumphs in 1986 and 1987. "It would be really nice to win that race," he said. "Round the circle a little bit.

"I hope it will work out that I'll have good form and I'll be leading the race and I'll tell my teammates how to work for me. But until that happens, I'll try to work for them. I want to set an example."

Directeur Sportif

TIME TO WORK — "*A lavoro,*" John Eustice said in Italian. Professional bicycle racers hear that all the time. The seven riders of the Amore & Vita team got to their feet, straddled their bicycles and began rolling toward the starting line.

"Have fun," Eustice called after them in English. Probably some other coach has said that to some team some place before. Perhaps it has even been said twice in the century that people have been racing bicycles. Eustice looked as if he said it often.

"One of my jobs is to keep them loose," he explained. "Europeans can come over here and feel displaced. I try to keep them happy."

He knew from long experience what keeps a racer happy. In 1975, at the age of 19, he became one of the first Americans to ride in Europe, starting with an amateur team in Italy. Before he retired as a professional in 1986, he had ridden for teams in Belgium, Germany, France, and Italy. In 1982, when he was a member of the respected Sem team in France, he won the U.S. professional championship. He repeated that feat in 1983.

"I went back to Europe with the star-spangled jersey on and tried to look impressive," he continued. "I didn't. Like a lot of guys, I had to work too hard for others instead of myself."

For the last decade, Eustice had been what he terms "an asterisk" in the sport: He organized races, including the former K-Mart Classic in West Virginia and the Olympic trials there; he ran training camps in Arkansas, New Jersey, and West

Virginia; he had been a technical consultant for ESPN at the last four Tours de France, and would be with the U.S. television network again in July.

Rider, organizer, agent, talent scout, analyst — until now, Eustice had done it all except serve as a *directeur sportif*. In the Tour DuPont, he headed Amore & Vita, a 16-man, second-division team in Italy that sent seven of its young riders to the United States.

Amore & Vita, which was then competing in Europe with its A team and officials, was looking for an American coach who knew racing and spoke Italian. Eustice, who had many important contacts in Italy, was looking for an opportunity. A holly grower in Ivyland, Pennsylvania, during the winter — "We move 20,000 pounds of holly in November and December, no bike talk allowed, got to be focused" — he had no crops to worry about in the spring.

"I was so nervous the first few days because I never did this before," he admitted. "Now it's better. It's rewarding doing this. I really like this job. I stayed away from it and now I find I love it. It's like going back into a cult."

As whistles blew and horns sounded for the fifth stage from Mount Airy, North Carolina, to Roanoke, Virginia, he slipped into the driver's seat of his team van and waited for a guest to move in beside him and a mechanic to get in the back before he began following the pack. The van was ninth in line among the 16 team vehicles, a ranking based on overall standings. Ahead were such major outfits as Motorola, Mapei, Festina, and Rabobank, and Amore & Vita's place was unexpectedly high.

Unexpected, that is, to anybody other than Eustice. With five first-year professionals and two second-year professionals, the team would not have been considered likely to place a man second in the stage into Richmond, third into Raleigh, North Carolina, and fifth into Greensboro, North Carolina. All those places had been taken by the team's sprinter, Glenn Magnusson.

The day before, just 700 meters from the finish in Greensboro, Magnusson was starting to fight it out for victory when his front wheel hit a pothole and cracked in two.

"Andriotto led him out," Eustice said, referring to Dario Andriotto. "He was fighting half the Mapei team to get position. Andriotto wouldn't have believed a week ago that he could ride equal against Mapei, but he does now."

To Eustice, his riders' results were easily explained: "A little team with a big spirit can give everybody else a hard time. We've got the spirit and we've got some talent too."

He did not add that Amore & Vita had an enthusiastic *directeur sportif* who was eager to see how far he could push his riders in 12 days and whether their accomplishments would shine some light on his own managerial skills.

"I'm a good coach," he decided. "I did everything wrong as a rider, that's why I'm a good coach. I can see things coming and say, 'Uh, uh, I lost three years that way.' I would give up everything else to run a team. I am good at building a team. Morale, excitement, that's what I'm good at.

"Like De Pasquale," he continued, referring to Maurizio De Pasquale, a strong climber. "I gave him the responsibility of team leadership. He was a little nervous at the beginning but now he's accepting it. I said, 'You're the team leader and you command in the field.'

"The first day, he came back and got water bottles and I said, 'Stop that. That's the last time you do that.' " The team captain, Eustice was saying, does not do the work of a support rider.

"He's there. Now he's getting used to his role, he likes it, he's starting to command the other guys. And they're happy listening. He's smart. He sees everything that's going on. Everything. And he's a good person. The guys listen to him. So he's the soul of the team right now."

How had Eustice decided to make De Pasquale his leader on such short acquaintance? "Observation," he explained. "Talent spotting. What I know."

The geographic profile of that day's stage in the DuPont lay on the dashboard of the team van that Eustice was driving, and marked in pencil were three points in the race where riders could win bonus money.

First came the sprint at tiny Stuart, Virginia: $5,000 for the first man through, $3,000 for the second and $2,000 for the third. The DuPont offered prizes of $200,000, including $35,000 to the winner, plus $64,500 in *primes*. In addition to the Stuart *primes*, the climb at Cahas would pay $1,000 to the winner and the climb at Lynville $1,000 more.

The overall winner when the stage finished in Roanoke, Virginia, would gain a *prime* of $2,500. That one was not marked on Eustice's map.

As *directeur sportif* of the young Amore & Vita team, he was being realistic. In Magnusson, a 27-year-old Swede, he had a sprinter who had already finished second, third, and fifth in DuPont stages, so there was some hope for the Stuart *prime*. In De Pasquale and Andrea Patuelli, both Italians, he had two climbers whom he thought capable of staying with the leaders in the Blue Ridge Mountains.

But really, he knew, he had no single rider who could both climb and sprint and contest the finish in Roanoke. In only his first week as a *directeur sportif* after a decade of experience as a rider, the 40-year-old Eustice knew how to balance bouyancy about his team with common sense.

"It's professional sports," he remarked. "There has to be a certain hardness about it."

So the Stuart sprint and its big money meant less to him than some other concerns. First was his worry that Magnusson might not make it over the first of four days in the mountains to contest the last few sprints before the DuPont ended in Marietta, Georgia.

"He'll see how he feels, whether he's strong or not, and if he doesn't feel like going for it at Stuart, he'll spend the next few days helping the others. They've been working hard for Magnusson and now he's got only the sprint today and the hope that he can make it over the mountains and some of the other sprinters don't."

Mile 17 of 110: Magnusson drops back in the pack and raises an arm for assistance. The Amore & Vita van pulls out of its ninth position among the 16 team cars and moves up on Magnusson's left. He looks weary. The metal plates on his shoe soles that lock into his pedals need some oil. While the mechanic in the back of the van opens the side door, leans out and tends to that, Eustice asks, "How you feeling?" The rider smiles, nods. "Good job, baby," the coach says.

Mile 24: Leon van Bon, a Dutchman with Rabobank and a sprinter who has already won a daily stage, easily wins the Stuart sprint. Serge Baguet, a Belgian with Vlaanderen 2002, is second and Michael Blaudzun, a Dane with Rabobank, is third. Despite the $10,000 *prime*, Magnusson has decided not to contest the sprint. "A lot of guys are tired," Eustice comments.

Mile 30: Filippo Meloni, an Italian with Amore & Vita, falls to the rear, signals for the van, passes in three empty water bottles and takes five full ones. He stuffs them into the pockets of his jersey and even into its neck. When he returns to the pack, he will distribute the water to his teammates on this hot and muggy day. "Hold on, do what you can do," Eustice instructs him in Italian. "He's exhausted and sick," the coach explains. "He's been raced too much this year and came here sick from the Tour of the Vaucluse in France. All he can hope to do in the DuPont is hang on."

Mile 38: Luca Maggioni, another Italian with Amore & Vita, signals for water, takes two bottles and rides off. "My problem child," Eustice says. "He's doing nothing in the race and I tell him to at least get water for the others but he just gets it for himself. That makes me so mad. And there's nothing I can do. Yesterday I was screaming at him. Oh boy, what can you do?"

Mile 50: Malcolm Elliott, an Englishman with Chevrolet L.A. Sheriff and a fine sprinter, pulls off to the right shoulder and stops. Since there has been just one small climb and he has not been left far behind, he must be quitting for other reasons, probably stomach troubles. "That's what we want," Eustice says, "get rid of the competition." He thinks about that. "You feel sorry for him, but that's racing."

Mile 52: Marcel Wust of the MX Onda team and Robbie McEwan of Rabobank, both sprinters, attack at the foot of the Sugarloaf Mountain climb and open a lead of 250 meters. "They're trying to get over the mountains," Eustice says. "It's a smart move — either that or a dumb move." He laughs.

Mile 56: The field shatters on the climb. Four Amore & Vita riders are left behind, three stay with the leaders. Eustice guns the van past his stragglers after giving each more water and a supportive word. He is heading for the first group and his three riders there. "Be tough, hang tough," he tells Maggioni.

Mile 58: Magnusson is in a small group behind the leaders. His eyes are glazed with the uphill effort. "Good boy, hang on," Eustice says, passing him two water bottles. "We have nobody to win the stage now," he says as he accelerates. "He's seen his limits. Now he knows how far he has to go."

The sky had been growing darker during the afternoon and now, with about seven miles to the finish, a thunderstorm erupted. Lightning flashed over nearby hills and hail began pelting the road. Far ahead, the race radio announced first that a small group including Lance Armstrong and Tony Rominger had broken away, then that Rominger had crashed on a left-hand turn made slick by the torrent and car oil on the road.

Eustice and his mechanic were interested in the news, if not overly. Their more immediate worries were how many of their riders would make it to Roanoke without crashing or finishing so far behind that they were disqualified.

In the end, everybody on the Amore & Vita team except Maggioni, the problem child, made it. He stopped during the storm, was picked up by the broom wagon, and spent the rest of the DuPont riding in the team's second van with mechanics, masseurs, and spare wheels.

Overall, four riders did not finish, and one other was disqualified for lateness. Armstrong won the stage and De Pasquale, the team captain and star climber, was the highest Amore & Vita finisher, 23rd, or 16 seconds behind. Patuelli, the team's other climber, was 30th, in the same time. Meloni, the sick rider, was 88th, or 20 minutes 50 seconds behind. Magnusson was 81st, or 13:22 behind.

Magnusson's lost time meant nothing to Eustice since his rider was concentrating on individual victories, not general classification. The *directeur sportif* cared only that, if Magnusson continued to get over the mountains, the team still had its sprinter available for the final stages. "He lives to fight another day," Eustice announced exultantly.

"It's so rewarding doing this," he added, his face alight. "I really like doing this. I get so crazy doing a race. I really love this job."

On Native Soil

WHEN THE HARDEST part was over in the Tour DuPont, the Blue Ridge Mountains crossed and left behind, Chann McRae was one of the few riders sorry to see them go. They represented a lost opportunity.

The U.S. national road race champion in 1992 and 1995, McRae is a good climber and usually rode strongly in the DuPont's mountains. In 1996, however, he struggled. "I guess I didn't recover too well from my earlier races," he said. "I'm toughing it out but it's been difficult."

Nevertheless, he was able to help his team in other ways. "I can read this race very well now," he said. "I tell my team director, 'OK, this is what's going to happen today' and usually it happens."

This was McRae's sixth DuPont and the first in which he did not wear the star-spangled jersey of the U.S. national team. Now he wore the teal and white of the Santa Clara team from Spain because, at age 24, McRae turned professional over the winter.

"That's what I always aspired to be," the native of Plano, Texas, said. "Uh huh. Since I was 18 years old. That seems a long time ago, but I didn't want to do it too early. I wanted to be one of the best amateurs before I turned pro. I won the national amateur championship last year and was first amateur, 19th place overall, in the DuPont. This year was the right time."

The Santa Clara team was based in Valladolid in north-central Spain and raced a heavily Spanish schedule. "In Spain it's all about mountains," he said. "If you can climb, you'll be there at the finish."

McRae had raced in the Semana Catalana and the Tours of Valencia and the Basque Country, plus a few one-day races, before he returned to the United States two weeks before the DuPont to train. He had finished as high as 19th twice in stages in his first year, and his big goal was the Vuelta a Espana in September.

"I have no desire to race much outside Spain right now," he said, "because the racing there is the best in the world. The sport is so serious there."

He first attracted Santa Clara's attention in the Tour of China the year before, when he finished eighth in the climb to the Great Wall. "I think I impressed them. I showed them that I have the potential to climb, and that's a necessity." Discussions went on during the winter before he signed and moved to Spain late in February.

"I talked to American teams too," he said, "and I was tempted. But I knew that if Santa Clara gave me a good offer, they're definitely the team I wanted to sign with. I wanted to race in Europe full-time. In Europe, I think you can progress and be a better rider.

"It's total professionalism with Santa Clara," he continued. "Everything is taken care of for you, and all you have to do is produce results. But it's not easy. In amateurism, you start fast and then the race eventually slows down. In the pros, it's faster, faster, faster, and the last two hours are even faster."

Before he made his decision, McRae talked it over with his childhood friend, former teammate with the U.S. national squad and sometimes training partner, Lance Armstrong.

"We talked all winter. He thought it was a really good opportunity," McRae reported. "He said if he was in a similar situation, he'd do the same thing."

Armstrong and McRae both lived now in Austin, Texas, and trained together twice a week during the winter. "I can't go out with him seven days a week," Armstrong said in a separate interview, "because he goes too hard, he trains too hard. He's one of those guys who think if he's not going hard, he's not doing enough.

"He's really serious — serious with his diet, never drinks any beer. He's very, very serious."

McRae told it somewhat differently. His version of their boyhood in Plano includes an animated social life and the time they were both expelled from Plano East Senior High School for absenteeism because of commitments to bicycle races.

"They kicked me and Lance out because we were always away so much. I was invited to try out for the junior national team and so was he. OK, it was a great opportunity. I went to training camp in California and he showed up in Colorado about one month later. So we missed about a month of school each and they wouldn't let us back in. They kicked both of us out. He ends up graduating from a private school in Plano and I ended up graduating from Palmer High School in Colorado Springs. So Plano East Senior High isn't even our alma mater. You would think they'd have been more supportive."

Their friendship, McRae continued, goes back to elementary school. "We've been competing against each other — cross country, triathlon, track and field, swimming, cycling — for years and years. We pushed each other to try different sports. But we used to do other things than just ride our bikes. We'd go out on the town, partying, meet girls."

Armstrong looked stunned when he was asked about this later.

"Don't listen to him, that's what I've got to say," he exclaimed. "I've known Chann for a long time, and here we are at the same level in the same sport. We both went through running, swimming, triathlete and cycling. But he didn't party. I partied. He's a home boy. He's serious, he's too serious."

Armstrong did agree, however, that McRae had a bright future. "I think he's talented," he said. "I think he's strong. It depends on what he wants to do, but he can have a very nice career."

A Victim of Downsizing

LIKE ANY VICTIM of corporate downsizing, Lance Armstrong seemed subdued and thoughtful as he examined his options after the Motorola electronics company announced that it would withdraw at the end of the 1996 season as a sponsor of the team he led.

The search had begun for a new sponsor, preferably a multinational company based in the United States willing to put about $5 million a year into one of the sport's stronger teams. Even though Armstrong did not have a guaranteed job for the next season, he knew that as a former world road-race champion, the winner of two stages in the Tour de France, a strong rider in the classics, and one soon to win the Tour DuPont for the second successive year, he would not have to start selling insurance on commission. Approaching his peak as he neared his 25th birthday, he seemed to be in a strong position in the market.

In fact, he admitted, although he preferred to stay in Motorola's blue and red, he had already had some preliminary contacts with European teams. "I started in April talking with teams," he said near the end of the DuPont. "I'm not saying who. Just feeling it out a little bit. Even if Motorola announced today they would do two more years, I don't have a contract beyond this season.

"So it's normal to talk to other teams. I have to figure out my value. But how much time do I have? Good question. I don't know. Space on teams goes fast. And money. That kind of money is not easy to come by. That's the reason I started in April. It's never too early."

He was believed to be making at least $750,000 that season and should have been eligible for a raise based on his superlative spring, including second place in Paris–Nice and Liège–Bastogne–Liège, and victory in the Flèche Wallonne and the DuPont. He ranked among the top 10 of the world's hundreds of professional riders.

Those results from somebody who said he despised the cold and rainy weather of spring races were no fluke. "This winter I was extremely motivated," he explained, "because I knew my contract was finished this year. I had a feeling Motorola wouldn't return. So, for 1997, to have to go out and maybe find a new team, find a new contract, find a new salary, I had to be super."

He also said that he had been changed by the death of his teammate Fabio Casartelli, after a crash in the Pyrenees in the previous Tour de France: "It did change me, it did. It changed everybody in the Motorola program, and I think it changed everybody in the sport to an extent. Now I realize that not only my career and my contract are precious, but your life is precious. At the same time that I was worried about not having a contract next year, he doesn't have a life any more.

"That was a really hard time. I still think of it, I do. I would be lying if I said I woke up every morning thinking of it. And if I said I thought about it every day, I would be lying. But I definitely think about it. You don't think of the event, you think more of the person.

"So it's something that makes you realize…" He faltered and tried again: "I always thought I was talented and strong and had ability and potential, and I trained hard, but I never did everything. Watching everything I ate and training even harder, not having beers and really focusing on the job. This winter I really did that. It's all tied into the contract, but it's also realizing that Fabio doesn't have that choice now and that I have to take advantage of what I have. It would be a shame if I didn't do all those things, because I can do good for the sport, for America, for a sponsor."

Although rumors had predicted that Motorola would drop out after six years as a sponsor, a long stay in the sport, the announcement came when the team was making its biggest impact.

"Obviously, results didn't factor into their decision," he said coldly. "They were never the sponsor to call up after a stage and say 'Why the hell didn't you win today?' They weren't the kind to call up before a race and say 'You've got to win today — the Tour DuPont, you've got to win five stages.' They were never that involved, so I don't know if results ever mattered to them."

What would Armstrong say about himself if, in his job search, he had to run a classified ad? "You mean like white single male seeks…?" he joked. "OK, this is what I would say: I can be competitive in classic races, hard classic races. I can be competitive in 7-to-10-day stage races. I can't guarantee you that I can win the Tour de France, I can't guarantee you that I can win field sprints, I can't guarantee you that I can win the climb to Alpe d'Huez, but I can certainly be a contender.

"And you have to remember that I'm only 24 years old. When I came into this sport as a pro, I was 21, and this is not a sport where you're peaked out at 21. It's a progressive sport up until a certain point, 29 or 30, so that's a big part of it as well."

If Jim Ochowicz, the Motorola team's general manager, could not find a new sponsor by the Tour de France, Armstrong said, then he would sign with another team. "If he tells me he thinks something's going to come through, then I can wait. Because I trust him.

"But if he comes to me and says I really can't find anything, which he would do, he would tell me, then I would go away immediately."

He seemed uncertain — his word was "open" — about where he would like to land if Motorola was through.

"No team is in, no team is out. I have to look at the direction, I have to look at the money, what they expect me to do. If they expect me to race from February to October, I'm probably not going to go there. It will have to be a competitive team, a team that will be supportive."

Armstrong had no doubts that, whoever he signed with, he would be the team leader and that he would be a good one. He had obviously thought often of his responsibilities in that role, even at 24, for Motorola.

"As soon as the leader sets the precedent, the others will follow," he explained. "That's always the sign of a good leader: When he comes on, when he's good, the others will rise.

"You have to be the leader of the guys in so many examples: doing the kilometers, at the dinner table when they're passing out desserts and you say no, if you're doing extra training, whatever, the guys will follow if they see their leader doing that. And as soon as they see his hard work begin to produce results, then it snowballs and gets bigger and better.

"I don't mind riding for the team. My time will come. My results will come. I know Lance Armstrong will have his day. So I don't have any stress about it. It's better for the team. Two big chiefs on a team fighting each other, that's no good. And I know that. I believe when anybody on the team wins, the whole team wins.

"I don't want to win everything, I don't. I think that's one of the first rules of cycling: You can't win everything. You can't be greedy," a flaw he had accused Laurent Jalabert of having.

"I cannot afford to be greedy. It's a political sport and you have to respect the others. If you are constantly trying to take away their victories, you have to be more of a gentleman. It sounds strange and I'm sure people don't understand it and think it goes against the laws of sports. I guess the best thing to say is you just can't be greedy.

"I've been last and I've been second and actually last feels worse. The ones who win a lot also get second. Look at Indurain, how many times has he been second in events? The big champions also get second place a lot. In this sport, I think, all you have to do is be there. If you're a rider that's always there, that's always in contention, is always competitive throughout the calendar year, or most of the year, you're a valuable rider, you're set.

"I just want to be consistent," he decided. "I want to be strong, I want to have a full career. I don't want to be a guy who's around a year or two and is gone. And I'm not. I feel I'm getting stronger."

6

The Tour de France

G AZING INTO HIS CRYSTAL BALL, Lance Armstrong saw all, knew all, but in 1996 told only some. The year before, when he offered a preview of the Tour de France, he told all: Miguel Indurain was unbeatable, even if Armstrong was troubled by the statistical possibility of five successive victories. The odds were against it, he said then, but he couldn't imagine — correctly, as it turned out — that anybody could challenge the Spaniard.

Now Armstrong was not so sure.

"Indurain, he'll be super. He knows what he's doing. Even though it will be difficult for him — he's lost a lot of strong guys" from his Banesto team, "you have to pick him, you just have to.

"But I'm holding out right now," Armstrong said early in the season, "because I've been staying in Monaco and doing some training with Tony Rominger. And, man, he thinks he can win it."

That was the same Tony Rominger who also thought he could win it other years, notably 1993, when he finished second by nearly five minutes, 1994, when he dropped out with shattered morale halfway through after Indurain left him far behind on the first mountain, and 1995, when he finished a listless eighth, nearly 17 minutes down. But it was also the same Rominger who won the Giro d'Italia in 1995 and the Vuelta a Espana from 1992 through 1994.

Which Rominger would show up for the start of the 3,800-kilometer Tour June 29 in the Netherlands? Armstrong was not sure.

"I was training with him and just flat out asked him: 'Tony, do you really think you can win the Tour de France, do you really think you can beat Indurain?' Because we'd been riding and talking, a pretty friendly conversation, we get along all right. So I said, 'Do you really think you can beat him?'

"And he tells me, 'Yes.' He really thinks he can. If things go right and he plans his season right and this, that and the other thing. And I said, 'How are you going to beat him?' I sort of had to answer it for him: Was he going to try to drop him on the climbs? It's difficult to do it in the time trials. I think he thinks he has to do it in the climbs and maybe the uphill time trial.

"But he thinks he can do it."

If so, Rominger would begin trying on July 6, the seventh stage after a week on the plains of Holland, Belgium and eastern France. The Tour entered the Alps that day on a 202-kilometer stage between Chambéry and Les Arcs that included three big climbs: the Madeleine, 20 kilometers with an average grade of 7.8 percent; the Cormet de Roselend, 20 kilometers at 6 percent, and Les Arcs, 14.7 kilometers at 7.8 percent.

The next day, stage eight, was a 30-kilometer individual time trial from Bourg St. Maurice up to Val d'Isère with half that distance on a grade of 5.9 percent. The day after that, July 8, a 190-kilometer stage from Val d'Isère to Sestriere, Italy, was scheduled, with these climbs: the Iseran, 15.5 kilometers at 5.8 percent; the Galibier, 34.7 kilometers at 5.4 percent; the Montgenèvre, 8.1 kilometers at 6 percent; and the final ramp to Sestriere, 10.8 kilometers at 6.1 percent.

The Alps concluded July 9 with a stage from Turin, Italy, to Gap, France, of 203 kilometers with two climbs: the Montgenèvre again, this time 42.4 kilometers at 3.1 percent, and the Sentinelle, 5.3 kilometers at 5 percent.

After a series of rolling stages through the Massif Central, the Tour would reach the Pyrenees on July 16, the 16th stage. It ended with a climb of the Hautacam, 13.4 kilometers at an average grade of 7.8 percent. The granddaddy of all mountain stages was scheduled the next day, July 17: 260 kilometers from Argelès-Gazost to Pamplona, Spain, over the Aubisque, 28.4 kilometers at 4.2 percent; the Marie Blanque, 8.7 kilometers at 7.1 percent; the Soudet, 15.8 kilometers at 6.8 percent; the Port de Larrau, 14.8 kilometers at 7.9 percent; and the Remendia Hill, 2.7 kilometers at 3.7 percent, before a long descent to Pamplona, the main city near the pueblo where Indurain grew up.

"The stage into Pamplona is certainly good for Indurain," Armstrong said. "You look at the Tour and you say, 'They're trying to work it against him,' and then they put an eight-hour stage into his hometown. That's not too mean."

The main difficulties between Pamplona and the finish in Paris on July 21 were expected to be the 18th stage, a series of short, steep climbs from Spain to Hendaye, France, and the final individual time trial, 60 more or less flat kilometers from Bordeaux to St. Emilion, on July 20.

Other than Indurain and Rominger, Armstrong foresaw no challengers for victory in the 83rd Tour.

"Who else would there be?" he asked. "Who?"

Chris Boardman, the Englishman who was Olympic pursuit champion, former world time-trial champion and former holder of the hour record? "No. Prologue, yeah. For the prologue, great, the favorite. But overall, no, no, no."

Evgeni Berzin, the Russian who won the 1994 Giro at age 24 and finished second in that race in 1995 before collapsing in the Tour and quitting early in the mountains? "No, definitely not. He has to prove himself first."

Laurent Jalabert, the Frenchman who finished fourth in the last Tour, won the 1995 Vuelta and then stood No. 1 in the computerized rankings of the world's top riders? "No. Can't time-trial well enough. We're talking about Indurain and Rominger — you can't beat them if you can't time trial."

Lance Armstrong, the American star, former world road-race champion and reigning Tour de France oracle? "No. He's not putting any emphasis on the Tour. It's only a preparation for the Olympics."

Who would have thought at that point to ask about Bjarne Riis or Jan Ullrich?

The Prologue

RACING IN A MISTY RAIN over slippery roads, the favorites and challengers began the Tour de France by deciding that a little prudence was acceptable but that only losers practice real caution.

They went all out over a short prologue course that would have been undemanding if not for a downpour during most of the afternoon. After that, the puddled roads were called treacherous by many of the early starters.

Even Chris Boardman, the British specialist in prologues, who crashed in the rain in the brief time trial that started the previous Tour, decided finally against prudence. In case of rain, he said a few days before the 83rd Tour began, "We take it steady. We're not taking any risks this year."

That was well spoken but not accurate. Although he did seem to coast through some tight curves, he posted a time of 10 minutes 55 seconds over the 9.4-kilometer course. Imagine if the roads had been dry.

For a while, Boardman had the fastest time. In the end, he had to settle for second place in the 197-man field as Alex Zülle, a Swiss who rode for the ONCE team and who finished second overall in the 1995 Tour, came home in 10:53. "When I saw the first riders on television, I realized that it was dangerous and I didn't imagine anybody would go as fast as we did," Zülle said afterward.

Third was Evgeni Berzin, a Russian with Gewiss who won the Giro d'Italia in 1994, in 10:56. Thereafter the honor roll comprised the rest of the big names: Abraham Olano, a Spaniard with Mapei and the world road-race champion, fourth; Tony Rominger, also with Mapei and the holder of the world record for the one-hour ride, fifth; Bjarne Riis, a Dane with Telekom and the third-place finisher in the previous Tour, sixth; Miguel Indurain, of Banesto and the winner of the last five Tours de France, seventh; and Laurent Jalabert of ONCE and the world's top-ranked rider, eighth.

And there you had what was widely regarded as the complete list of possible winners of the world's richest, toughest and most prestigious bicycle race. The prologue, in which riders started alone a minute apart, was the first step in the

3,900 kilometers (2,423 miles) to be covered before the Tour would end July 21 in Paris.

Boardman, who started seventh from last, was drained afterward and speechless as he watched the electronic times of those, including Zülle, who had started after him.

The Briton, the leader of the Gan team, thus passed the first of what he expected to be many "challenges" in the Tour de France. Not difficulties, problems, hurdles or obstacles, but challenges — he was thinking as positively as he could.

Boardman learned this trick from a sports psychologist and had tried to apply it in the previous Tour. But, not even five minutes into the start of the race, he crashed in the rain, breaking his left ankle and right wrist. His season was over.

Now he had returned in splendid form. If not for the rain, he would have been the favorite in the prologue when the 83rd Tour began in 'sHertogenbosch, a cordial Dutch city whose name translates as "The Duke's Woods." Also known as Den Bosch in the same way some people refer to Philadelphia as Philly, the city was spending about $1.75 million for the publicity it hoped to get as host for the short prologue and the next day's long first daily stage.

But all that money could not buy sunny weather.

"I hope it doesn't rain," Boardman had said earlier in an impromptu news conference after his Gan team completed the perfunctory medical inspection that all riders attend to prove they have a pulse.

And if it did rain? "We take it steady," Boardman replied, wrongly, as it happened. "We're not taking any risks this year. I can't afford to crash out again, I can't afford that.

"The mistake I made last year was small, but in those conditions and at 80 kilometers an hour, the consequences were quite catastrophic. I can't afford to lose another year. I lost a year and can't do that again. I need the experience of a three-week race. It's more important to me than to win a prologue."

Time was pressing for Boardman, who would turn 28 in August and did not become a professional until he was 25.

Even if the sun had been out, however, the prologue was not his main goal.

That, he explained, was finishing the Tour. "The first thing is Paris. I find that a big challenge, and that's how I'm trying to think of it — as a challenge. It's quite scary, you know, the fact that you're riding a race so long that you have to have a haircut in the middle."

Having dropped out ill halfway through the 1994 Tour and having crashed the next year, Boardman had never completed more than a 10-day race.

What he wanted to know was whether he had the stamina to win the Tour once a new wave of riders succeeded Indurain. Therefore, Boardman said, finishing the race was of prime importance. "If I can win the prologue and take the yellow jersey, that would be super — it would take pressure off me," he continued. "If I could have one good day in the mountains, with a ride at the front, and I could win the prologue and arrive in Paris — top 20 is a reasonable objective — then that would be a great Tour for me. A super Tour. That would be progression."

Most people had him pegged for a better finish than top 20, but Boardman was reluctant to speculate.

"Everybody keeps biting off more than I can chew," he joked. "I think it's best to finish the Tour first before I say what I can do. Maybe it's possible to do better, but you need absolutely perfect form for this race. And at the moment I'm not confident I'm in perfect form. I just finished antibiotics on Tuesday for a nose infection and I just don't feel fantastic.

"I was training in the mountains, climbing the Galibier," an Alpine peak that was to be part of the ninth stage, "and I was sort of tired doing it. That's a climb 27 miles long, two hours, and that's one of four or five that day. I'm well aware of the challenges to come and that's why I don't want to speculate on what I can achieve.

"I certainly don't feel bad — I'm in good shape — but I don't have that euphoric feeling that I've had in the past. So I hope it will be enough for the prologue and there won't be too many challenges the first week."

There was that word again: "challenges."

Stage One

IF HE SPOKE ENGLISH, he would call himself Super Mario. Or try the Italian Stallion. Instead, Mario Cipollini had to make do with Il Magnifico, the Magnificent One, or, because of his tawny ponytail and constant two-day stubble, the Re Leone, the Lion King. Cipollini — little onion in Italian — preferred Il Magnifico, of course. Who wouldn't?

Then 29 years old and the leader of the Saeco team in the Tour de France, Cipollini had been acknowledged for the last few years as the best sprinter in bicycle racing, and certainly the flashiest.

Flash: After a daily stage of the Tour of Catalonia in June 1996, he denounced the race's organizers for, he charged, treating the riders like cattle, housing them in hotels so mean that there was no drinkable water, and providing no pasta at meals. He would never return to the race, he said, adding that this was a shame since he adored his fans in Spain and they, of course, adored him.

Best: He spoke immediately after he had won his third stage in the week-long race.

Flash: While everybody else on his team wore the uniform black shorts in the Italian championships the week before, Cipollini wore bright red ones.

Best: He did win the championship, of course, in a sprint, of course. It was his 15th victory of the season, highest in the sport, all of them sprints.

Flash: He wore scarlet shorts again — they look natty with the green, white, and red of the Italian flag on Cipollini's new jersey as the national champion — in the prologue of the Tour de France. For that offense against decorum, the race organizers fined him 50 Swiss francs ($40) and his team director 250 Swiss francs. Defiantly, Cipollini wore the red shorts again the next day, Stage One.

Best: Not quite. He was judged to have interfered with another rider in the tumultuous sprint and was dropped from third place to 37th after 209 kilometers out of, around and back into the host city of 'sHertogenbosch. Even Il Magnifico can't be magnificent all the time.

Not that he didn't try.

He was well placed at the front by his Saeco teammates, three of them bruisers more than six feet tall and immovable in the scuffling that goes on just before the finish. Cipollini was driving for what he thought was victory until, in the last 75 meters, Frédéric Moncassin, a Frenchman with the Gan team who had been boxed in, came around the Italian on the right and passed the line first.

Moncassin was timed in 5 hours 1 second for the race in strong winds, occasional rain and daylong dark clouds. When he painted those blue Dutch skies, Vermeer must have been using a vivid imagination.

Second, in the same time, was Jeroen Blijlevens, a Dutchman with TVM, and third was Jan Svorada, a Czech with Panaria — not the penalized Cipollini. Zülle retained the yellow jersey, while Berzin moved up to second place overall and Olano moved up to third, as Boardman finished 15 seconds behind them.

The first of 21 daily stages was watched by an immense crowd that the police estimated at more than a million of the 17 million Dutch. To most veteran observers of the Tour, it was the largest crowd ever seen all along a day's route.

Spilling onto narrow roads and leaving only a thin trail for the racers to pass through, the fans made the stage resemble the traditional one at Alpe d'Huez, a favorite with the Dutch. But this was a mountain stage without mountains.

Cipollini was in his element since the roads, as flat as a filleted North Sea herring, guaranteed a sprint finish. He escaped the half dozen crashes among nervous riders on a route laced with traffic islands and speed bumps — "*Let Op,*" watch out, the signs warned. Letting op was what the riders tried to do under the crowded and occasionally rainy condition. Nevertheless, the crashes claimed a few victims: Djamolidine Abdoujaparov, the Uzbek now riding for Refin, was knocked out; Frankie Andreu, one of Motorola's Americans, tore up his left thigh; Thierry Marie, a Frenchman with Agrigel, missed a turn around a traffic island and butted a sign with his helmeted head; Hernan Buenahora, a Colombian with Kelme and the most aggressive rider in the previous Tour, had to abandon after he broke a finger in a crash. "This shouldn't be allowed," complained Luc Leblanc, a Frenchman with Polti, after he lost many minutes due to crashes. "They're playing with our health," he said of the organizers.

Only 37 riders were still at the front when they came to the sprint finish after the entirely flat stage. Most of the first week of the three-week Tour promised to be equally accommodating for sprinters, since it would be, as tradition dictates, over flat, or no worse than rolling, territory. This period before the climbing begins is where the sprinters shine.

Ordinarily, Cipollini would shine brightest.

"He's the best," said Lance Armstrong. "And he's good for cycling. His personality and his character, they keep people interested in cycling. Cipo, he's got the hair, he's got the talk, he's got the scruffy face — he's got everything. Well, not everything, but he sure has a real personality."

Probably, but in his previous three Tours de France, Cipollini had not been dominating, having won three stages — as many as he won in the 1996 Giro d'Italia. He is usually tired, he says, after the Giro, where he goes all out as the Italian leader of an Italian team in his country's biggest race. Also, the competition and pressure are a notch higher in the Tour.

"There are a lot of good sprinters," Cipollini said in a brief interview before the first stage. Were there any he feared? "There are a lot of good sprinters," he repeated.

But he was the best, no? "If you say so," he replied. "But you're saying it, not me." Il Magnifico seemed unaccustomedly reserved.

How well did he hope to do in the first week? "My best." Meaning victory? "My best possible. Victory depends also on my teammates, luck, the course, destiny." He must have suspected something, for the Lion King did not intend to roar.

Stage Two

THIS TIME, Il Magnifico lived up to his name. Mario Cipollini, the Magnificent One, easily won the sprint finish in the second stage, a day after he came in third and then was bounced down to 37th place for interfering with another rider.

Convoyed to the front of the pack by his Saeco teammates, a burly bodyguard worthy of a South American generalissimo, Cipollini stayed in a straight line for the last 300 meters and crossed the finish a winner by a bicycle length.

He beat the same three sprinters involved in the previous day's *contretemps* — Blijlevens, Svorada and Moncassin — threw his arms into the familiar V signal, clasped his hands overhead and beamed.

"I'm very happy," the Italian said shortly afterward, "because this makes up for yesterday. I'm sorry if I didn't pay attention then to where other riders were."

He was not so chastened that he neglected to wear the outlawed red shorts for which he was paying a daily fine of 50 Swiss francs for violating the Tour's idea of a dress code. If his teammates all wore black shorts, the reasoning went, so should he, even if the red shorts Cipollini wore did look adorable with the green, white and red jersey of the Italian national champion.

So unapologetic was he, in fact, that he promised to wear green shorts if he gained the green points jersey that he first wore in 1994, and even yellow ones if he donned the yellow jersey of the overall leader.

Until that fashion breakthrough, the yellow jersey continued to be worn by Zülle. Second was Moncassin, one second behind after he won a six-second bonus sprint en route. Berzin was third, two more seconds behind. In 20th place overall, Cipollini was only 36 seconds away from his impersonation of the Sun King.

But he proved that he could be just as gracious as Louis XIV. "My wife has reproached me for dedicating my victories to everybody else except her," he said. "So I owe her this one, especially since living with someone like Mario Cipollini is very difficult."

Second in the 247.5-kilometer stage from tidy 'sHertogenbosch in the Netherlands to grimy Wasquehal in northern France was Blijlevens, who was given the same time of 6 hours 29 minutes 22 seconds as the winner. Svorada was third and Moncassin fourth.

This second stage began in a light drizzle that quickly turned into a downpour as the riders navigated on more narrow roads past verdant pastures — everything is green in a land with a water table as high as the Netherlands'. By the time the race crossed into Belgium and wider roads, the rain was only intermittent under a sky full of thunderheads. The main enemy was a constant headwind that bent saplings, shook the full heads of bigger trees, and kept the speed of the stage to a relatively slow 38 kilometers an hour.

Although the 194 riders remaining in the race knew the wind would impede them, an attack formed about Kilometer 112. Five riders went first, were joined by five more, and the 10 shook themselves out into a group of six and then four.

Those four included the Belgian Johan Museeuw of Mapei, the Dutchman Leon van Bon of Rabobank, and the Australian Neil Stephens of ONCE, all big motors, although Stephens was protecting the interests of his leader, Zülle, and did no work.

Museeuw was especially eager to keep the breakaway going since he was passing through the Flemish-speaking part of Belgium, his homeland, and he was wearing the black, yellow, and red jersey of the Belgian national champion.

The group's lead swiftly mounted to a peak of 6:20 after 30 kilometers before the pack decided that the foreordained end of the stage over flat terrain was a sprint finish. Across Belgium the chase continued, and down came the lead.

By Kilometer 184, the breakaway was caught. Nothing ventured, nothing gained, Museeuw said later.

Over the last 30 kilometers, a number of other riders tried their luck singly or in pairs. None succeeded. Once the pack crossed the border into France, Cipollini's teammates went to the front and raised the speed to inhibit other attacks and prepare for the sprint.

In the last kilometer, Slava Ekimov, a Russian with Rabobank, made the final attempt to escape. Once he was reeled in, Cipollini's vanguard peeled off and left the running to him.

Il Magnifico made no mistakes. The Lion King showed them all, even the Tour's committee in charge of color of shorts, just who ruled this jungle.

Stage Three

THE AUBERVILLIERS 93 team had racked up a number of firsts in its initial Tour de France: first rider to start the prologue, first to attack, and, in a three-way tie, first to crash.

If those were distinctions at all, they were minor ones, but they still would have been enough to draw dozens of the team's supporters 20 minutes by car north from the Paris working-class suburb of Aubervilliers to Nogent sur Oise, where the Tour finished its third stage.

The fans were watching their tax dollars — francs, actually — at work. The young team, then in its third year, was one of the few to be supported primarily by a municipality in a sport dominated by commercial sponsors.

Eager to prove they belonged in the Tour, the Aubervilliers 93 riders had done more in the race than simply show up since the prologue. The day before, for example, Frenchman Cyril Saugrain, one of the young team's better riders, had won a bonus sprint worth 100,000 Belgian francs (about $3,300). Another Aubervilliers 93 rider, Christophe Capelle, had finished fifth in the final sprint.

For the third stage, the team placed no one in the top 20 but did mount the only attack, by Laurent Genty in the first four and a half hours of a sluggish, 195-kilometer stage from Wasquehal south past World War I battlefields in Picardy to Nogent sur Oise. The stage, which was expected to last no more than five hours at its slowest, took half an hour more in continuing wind and occasional rain. The speed was a leisurely 35.5 kilometers an hour over flat terrain.

At the finish Erik Zabel, a German with Telekom, held off Cipollini to win by half a bicycle length. Zabel, who had been fifth and sixth in the two previous days' sprints, took the lead with about 200 meters to go and refused to fade as Cipollini charged on his right up a slight incline.

Third in the mass sprint was Moncassin, who used the eight bonus seconds he received to move into first place overall, the goal he had been pursuing nervously for three days. "On Sunday, Fred asked for a wheel change three times," his Gan *directeur sportif*, Roger Legeay, reported. "He said the tires were either too soft or too hard, but in fact they were all the same. On Monday, he was all wound up and went from too far out in too big a gear." This time he got it right, donning the jersey in Nogent, his wife's home town and the residence of her parents.

Moncassin moved seven seconds ahead of Zülle, whose ONCE team was happy to be rid of the pressure of protecting the man in the yellow jersey this early in the Tour. No climber, Moncassin was not expected to hold the jersey past the first day in the Alps, if that long.

But his triumph was loudly celebrated by the thousands of French fans at the finish. They are not accustomed to seeing one of their own in the yellow jersey.

That sorry state was part of the reason that the Tour for the first time included Aubervilliers 93, a team with an annual budget of 6.5 million French francs (about $1.3 million) in a sport where the major teams spend five, six and seven times more. Budget aside, Aubervilliers 93 was far from being a major team.

It was really a club of amateur riders who turned professional in 1994 — the 93 does not stand for the date but for its *département*, or administrative region, which is also one of its sponsors. As a second-division French team, it comprised mainly young hopefuls and a few veterans to show the others the ropes.

The world's greatest bicycle race admitted Aubervilliers as a sort of hamburger helper, to stretch the number of French riders participating. Although there might be four major French teams for the 1997 season, there was just one, Gan, at the start of 1996. Then Festina, a French-Italian team, transferred from Andorra to France, making it two French teams.

That added up to 14 riders from the mother country on domestic teams and 8 more on foreign teams, or 22 among the 198 riders on 22 teams. The total was an embarrassment to the Tour's organizers, who issued invitations to both Aubervilliers and Agrigel-La Creuse, another second-division French team, to bring the total to 38.

The number became second only to the 62 Italian riders participating and far ahead of the 23 Spaniards, in third place. Compared to the three riders from the United States, two from Britain and one each from Uzbekistan, Kazakhstan, and Venezuela, 38 even looked impressive.

It wasn't. Hard times continued for the sport of bicycle racing in France, its birthplace. With the economy pinched by an unemployment rate over 12 percent, sponsors were slow to step forward. Worse, five riders were reported positive in drug testing the month before the Tour started and two of them — Jacky Durand and Thierry Laurent, both of Agrigel — were riding in this Tour because the French Cycling Federation would not meet until July 15 to decide their suspensions. (They were banned for eight months each nearly two months later.)

In the Tour itself, no French rider had won since 1985, when Bernard Hinault did, and no Frenchman had even stood on the final three-step podium in Paris since 1989, when Laurent Fignon did.

So Moncassin's yellow jersey would be headline news and Aubervilliers 93 got its chance. Perhaps its riders' enthusiasm would compensate for their inexperience.

"We're very happy to be here, really we're delirious," said Saugrain, who turned 23 a month before. "We never expected this to happen. We're not a very important team, you know. Have you heard of us before?" he wondered.

Stage Four

THE TOUR DE FRANCE, so quiet since its start, suddenly exploded as it turned east and began heading toward what was supposed to be its first big rendezvous in the Alps in three days.

That turned out to be a few days late. After a five-man breakaway lasted 194 kilometers and finished 4 minutes 33 seconds ahead of the pack, the Tour had a new leader and, unlike Moncassin, an authentic one.

He was Stéphane Heulot, then a 25-year-old Frenchman with the Gan team, who climbed and time-trialed strongly. Right behind Heulot in the overall standings was another but lesser threat to the Tour favorites, Mariano Piccoli, also 25, an Italian with Brescialat who had won the best climber's jersey in the last two Giros d'Italia. He did not time-trial nearly as well as he climbed.

The French national champion, Huelot finished fourth in the Dauphiné Libéré in the Alps the month before, trailing only Miguel Indurain, Tony Rominger, and Richard Virenque, all Tour contenders. And he now held a cushion of more than four minutes before the race entered the mountains.

"Does that make me an outsider for victory in the Tour?" Heulot asked, repeating a question. "No," he decided. "Not really."

He was right, since this was his first Tour de France and he knew nothing of the pressures to come, let alone the differences in physical demands between an eight-day race like the Dauphiné and a three-week one like the Tour.

Those pressures and difficulties include long breakaways by opponents, like the one on this fourth stage. Riding in rare sunlight but continuing strong winds, the five set off at Kilometer 38 of the 232-kilometer stage from Soissons, through Champagne territory, to the park of Lac de Madine in Lorraine.

The five were Saugrain; Rolf Jaermann, a Swiss with MG; Danny Nelissen, a Dutchman with Rabobank, Heulot, and Piccoli. They built a lead that peaked at 17 minutes 20 seconds, watched it descend as the pack finally gave chase over rolling terrain in winds that changed from frontal to the sides, and finally steadied to finish 4:33 ahead.

In the sprint, the winner was Saugrain, 23 and in his first Tour with a team that ranked in the French second division. Just yesterday he had asked if his Aubervilliers 93 team had ever been heard of. It had now.

Saugrain led out the sprint about 500 meters from the line, looked back twice and saw that he was indeed holding off Nelissen, Jaermann, Heulot and Piccoli, in that order. Arms above his head and a broad smile on his face, Saugrain was timed in 5 hours 43 minutes 50 seconds, an average speed of 40.4 kilometers an hour.

The main pack of 188 riders remaining in the Tour staged a sprint of their own for sixth place, including a crash that decked Svorada, the wearer of the green points jersey. He appeared not to be seriously hurt.

Heulot now held the yellow jersey by 22 seconds over Piccoli and 34 seconds over Saugrain. The major contenders, Indurain, Rominger, Zülle, Jalabert, Riis and company, were at least 4:16 behind.

The new leader was merely protecting the interests of his teammate Moncassin when he joined the breakaway: Strategy dictates that a member of the man in the yellow jersey's team join an attack in the rare case that it builds a huge lead and a new overall leader results. If so, the hope is that it will be the teammate — the script for the fourth stage.

As the five whirled along narrow roads through Champagne's towns and fields and then into the farmland of Lorraine, Heulot rode at the rear in the others' slipstream, refusing to help in the relays, again as team strategy dictates. Only with 40 kilometers to go did he begin working at the front.

At that point, his Gan team officials in a nearby car decided that the breakaway had a real chance, not only of success but also of big success — 4 minutes 33 seconds is a major chunk of time — and decided that it did not matter to them who from the team was in the yellow jersey. Since Heulot was the highest ranked of the five in least elapsed overall time, if the breakaway's lead exceeded 40 seconds, and if he beat Piccoli for the bonus seconds, he would become the Tour's new leader.

It did, he did, and he did.

The main question now was how long Heulot could resist. The Tour had seen many young riders take the yellow jersey on more or less a fluke and wear it for no more than a day or two in the Alps.

Still, Heulot was considered one of the brightest French hopes when he turned professional in 1992. He lost his edge when he rode for two years with the Banesto team in Spain, which was headed by Indurain, before he joined Gan in 1996.

To the question of what he learned with Banesto, Heulot dismissively answers "Spanish." After he donned the yellow jersey, he was asked what he learned from Indurain and he was more respectful: "I learned to be calm and patient, like him, I hope."

Heulot had another few words about Indurain: "I spoke with Miguel and he told me that if everything went according to plan, he would take the yellow jersey from me after Bordeaux," or at the second time trial. They were both whistling past the graveyard.

Stage Five

ALONG WITH THE other 184 other riders left in the Tour de France, Lance Armstrong rode languidly due south on stage five, heading toward the Alps and a long weekend of climbing.

Down Departmental Route 33 from the start in the Lac de Madine park they came, along Route 164 in the Vosges region, finishing the 242-kilometer fifth stage into the city of Besançon on twisty and narrow Route 70. In heavy headwinds and frequent drenching rain, Armstrong was concentrating on those roads, of course, but part of his mind was on another thoroughfare: Peachtree Street in Atlanta. That would be the hub of the bicycle road race in the Olympic Games.

The Texan was focused on that 221.8-kilometer race on July 31, just 10 days after the Tour ended in Paris.

"Obviously that's what makes the most sense for me as a goal," he said, referring to the Games, in which he was also scheduled to ride in the time trial on Aug. 3. "They're in America and they're the Olympics — the combination is big. I'm looking forward to them, yes I am."

The Games in Atlanta would be the first ones open to professional riders, many of whom competed in the Olympics before as amateurs. Armstrong did, in

Barcelona in 1992, and finished 14th in a road race in which he was a favorite. Right afterward he turned professional with Motorola and went on to win two stages in the Tour de France. He then ranked fourth in the world on a computerized list of racers.

But, he warned, nobody should have expected him to shine in the overall standings in the 83rd Tour de France. He started the fifth stage in 54th place, 5 minutes 3 seconds behind. "Now is my time to lay low and prepare," he said. "In Atlanta and the World Cup races in August, the spotlight will be on me but it isn't right now."

It surely wasn't on the fifth stage, except for the moment after a mass crash when, on global television, he waved a fist at another rider, Gilles Bouvard of Lotto, presumably encouraging him to be more vigilant. Otherwise Armstrong was another face in the crowd as Jeroen Blijlevens easily won the sprint finish over Moncassin and Zabel.

Blijlevens was timed in 6 hours 55 minutes 53 seconds, a desultory average of 34.9 kilometers an hour. Because of the headwind, which gusted up to 40 kph, and the treacherously wet roads, the start was advanced by 15 minutes and the next day by 30 minutes in an effort to get everybody to the dinner table before what had become the norm of 10 P.M.

For some teams, it was even worse. Thierry Bourguignon of Aubervilliers 93 complained that "I got a massage at 11 the other night, after dinner, because the finish was so late. It's worse than ever before." The riders were increasingly loud in blaming the Tour's organizers for late starts and finishes to accommodate television coverage. "The late finishes aren't doing the riders, the team staff, or the press any favors," Armstrong said. "It means you have far less time to recover." Next to last word to Zülle: "If they carry out their plan to finish Tour stages even later next year, neither ONCE nor Zülle will be at the start," he told *l'Equipe*. Last word to Bourguignon, in the paper *France Soir*: "We know we are just pawns."

Overall, Heulot continued to wear the yellow jersey with a 20-second lead over Piccoli. All the favorites finished in the same time as the winner.

A familiar face and pair of scarlet shorts were missing from the sprint finish, though. Cipollini did not start, choosing instead to go home and continue training in the sun, not the Tour's rain, for his major goal: Like Armstrong, he was concentrating on the Olympic road race.

The American, however, said that he wanted to do his preparatory work in the Tour. While he did not intend to ride for a high place in the general classification — "no, no, no, absolutely not," he said — Armstrong listed definite objectives in the 3,900-kilometer race.

"I'll ride all the time trials 100 percent," he said, "not go very deep in the mountains and try to select stages to do something, mainly in the second half."

He added that he did not feel under any pressure to prove anything in the Tour for a prospective new employer before the season ended and Motorola dropped its sponsorship. "If what I've done doesn't impress a sponsor, what can I do next?" he asked.

"I think we've got a very good Tour team and I'll do all I can to help my teammates." He singled out Laurent Madouas, a Frenchman, as Motorola's brightest hope in the overall standings, not himself.

"It's fair to say I'm looking ahead to the Olympics, but certainly I recognize the importance of the Tour de France, its magnitude," Armstrong continued. "I'm not here to be just trying, I'm not here on vacation. I'm ready."

His physical condition, he reported, was "probably about 75 percent." After his easy DuPont victory in May, he went back to Austin, Texas, moved into his new home — "It's beautiful. I'm happier in it than I expected and I expected to be very happy" — and took a month off.

"Mentally that was good for me," he said, "physically I probably relaxed a little too much. I did train, but as every week went by, I could feel my condition getting worse and worse. I just wasn't putting in the hours I needed to maintain my condition." He blamed "a little bit of burnout" after his busy and successful spring racing.

The Tour overview done with, Armstrong returned to the Olympic race. "It's not the best course for me," he judged. "It's just not challenging, not super-challenging." The course was flat, with one small climb, although Atlanta's heat and humidity in the afternoon race were expected to be major factors.

"I don't think the course will be very selective," Armstrong continued, meaning that weaker riders would not be weeded out early. "It'll be more random and tactical. Which is unfortunate in such a big event, but they're not going to change it. I'll have to do what I can."

Stage Six

AS THUNDER ROARED and rain pelted down for another day, Lance Armstrong decided early in the sixth stage that an overnight sickness had robbed him of his power and that he could not continue in the Tour.

"I couldn't breathe," he said after his withdrawal. "I started feeling a little sick last night. I'm never sick and I didn't tell anyone I was sick. I'm bummed," he said, looking weary and depressed, nowhere near his usual ebullient self. "If I'm sick, I'm sick and I have to stop."

The first hour of the stage, he continued, was easy. "Then it started going hard and I had no power. I couldn't breathe." Armstrong fell behind the pack just before the second of five climbs over hills in the Jura and Savoy regions in eastern France. The sixth stage lasted 207 kilometers from Arc et Senans to the lakeside resort of Aix les Bains, usually in sight of the Alps across the water. But not this day, not with the curtains of rain whipped by heavy wind.

Once he dropped back in the gloom, Armstrong raised a hand to signal for his Motorola team car. When it arrived, Jim Ochowicz, the team's general manager, asked him if he wanted teammates to drop back and help tow him to the pack. Armstrong declined because he knew he would not make it to the finish even with help. The rear lights of the team car disappeared up the road.

He struggled on alone for about 20 kilometers before he coasted to the side of the road and stopped. An official removed the number 61 pinned on the back of his jersey, and Armstrong was officially out of the race. He remounted his bicycle, turned and rode back down the road, away from the other riders, knowing that another team car was far back and that he could get a ride in it to the team's hotel and not have to endure what he considered the ignominy of sitting all day in the broom wagon.

The next morning he was gone, getting a ride to Geneva and a plane from there back home to Texas. He carried on with his Olympic training in the hills around Austin and a scattered few races in the West and Midwest — hardly the rigorous preparation his major rivals were having in the Tour.

For Armstrong, this was the third time in his four Tours de France that he had not made it to the finish line, although the first two withdrawals were programmed because of his age and inexperience. The year before had been the sole time he finished, in 36th place.

He was not the only man to drop out. Weeklong rains and strong winds had forced the riders to strain in high gears, producing an epidemic of knee injuries in addition to the general weariness after late finishes, late massages, and late meals. In all, 13 riders, including Saugrain, quit during the stage, two did not start, and three finished outside the time limit and were disqualified, reducing the original field of 198 to 169 — with the mountains still to come. "I thought it was March," Heulot said after he donned a new yellow jersey. "I don't know how long we can take this." The forecast was for more rain and even for snow, at high altitudes, where the Tour was heading in the Alps.

The sixth stage was predictably the last big sprint for some days. Despite a long breakaway by four riders, about half the shredded pack rode together the last 37 kilometers and splashed along a bank of the Bourget Lake to the final line. Shortly before reaching it, Michael Boogerd, a Dutchman with the aggressive Rabobank team, which had been attacking near the finish on almost every stage, took a short lead and widened it as a chaser, Melchor Mauri, a Spaniard with ONCE, slid into the crowd barriers on a treacherous left turn. Boogerd won by a couple of bicycle lengths in the time of 5 hours 5 minutes 38 seconds, a rapid average of 40.6 kph despite the rain.

Second was Zabel, and third was Jalabert, who had sprinted for an earlier time bonus. The seconds he gained moved him ahead of Indurain in the general classification and meant that, if nothing changed, he would start the time trial in two days after the Spaniard. Ordinarily that would not have meant much, but this was not an ordinary Tour. "Miguel's motor works on solar energy," said José Miguel Echavarri, Banesto's *supremo*, of his star rider. Translated from the Spanish, that meant Indurain did not have much of a motor.

Stage Seven

IN A RARE SIGHT in the Tour de France, Miguel Indurain cracked on the final climb in the first day in the Alps, and struggled in so far behind many of his rivals at the finish in Les Arcs that his chances for a sixth successive victory in the race seemed seriously compromised.

Not since the start of the decade, when he was still a young support rider for Pedro Delgado, had the Spaniard fallen apart so totally. He could not stay with a main group of riders for the last few kilometers of the final 14.5-kilometer-long uphill ramp, and dropped farther and farther behind as he rode alone. At the end, he lost 4 minutes 19 seconds to the winner, and more than three minutes to his main foes.

He rode the last few kilometers in what looked like a trance, even accepting a soft drink from another team car, knowing he would be penalized because it was so close to the finish, where feeding by a *directeur sportif* is forbidden. (Indurain's team paid the fine of 500 Swiss francs ($400) levied on Emanuele Bombini, the Gewiss coach, for supplying the soft drink.) Desperate for sugar, Indurain flung away in disgust a water bottle graciously passed to him earlier by Alex Zülle as they climbed together. The Spaniard was not thirsty — he was starving.

The shock of his collapse was even greater since Indurain had passed over the first two mountains at the front, in second and then fifth place, and the ultimate climb was gently curving, not stunningly steep, terrain. "For the first 100 kilometers, I felt fine," Indurain said, "and even thought about attacking. Then, at Les Arcs, it was all different."

His collapse was one of many shocks during the 199-kilometer journey in occasional rain and cold fog from Chambéry over three big ascents to the resort of Les Arcs. Others included the withdrawal in tears of the man in the yellow jersey, Heulot, because of tendinitis in his right knee, an injury that had been kept secret; two crashes on a rapid mountain descent by Zülle that left him aching and uncertain; a spectacular launch off the road and into a ravine by Johan Bruyneel, a Belgian with Rabobank, from which he emerged mainly unhurt; and the shattering of Jalabert, Zülle's ONCE teammate and the supposed main rival to Indurain, on the first climb. All in all, it was one of the epic days in the 93-year history of the Tour de France, as those disasters are measured.

The sixth stage was won by Luc Leblanc, a bad boy of French racing who rode for the Polti team. A former world road-race and French national champion, Leblanc had often been criticized for his selfishness and his willingness to betray teammates in order to win a race himself. (Leblanc would not have thought, like Zülle, to pass a water bottle to his opponent; there was no chivalric code in the sport for Leblanc, who did not realize that without the code, bicycle racing was no more than a bunch of men in short pants pedaling.) Nobody could find any fault with his performance this day, however. He finished in feeble sunlight in 5 hours 47 minutes 22 seconds, a swift average of 34.5 kilometers an hour over two first-category climbs and one climb — 19.5 kilometers over the 6,562-foot-high Madeleine Pass — so long, steep and difficult that it was rated beyond category.

Forty-seven seconds behind the winner was Tony Rominger, who crashed heading for the Cormet de Roselend and was paced back, looking wobbly, to the main group and his strong finish. Peter Luttenberger, an Austrian with Carrera, was third, 52 seconds behind Leblanc. Fourth, fifth, and sixth, in the same time as Luttenberger, were Richard Virenque, a Frenchman with Festina; Laurent Dufaux, a Swiss with Festina; and Abraham Olano of Spain, riding for Mapei.

All except Rominger, who was 35 years old, were under 30. Leblanc was 29 and the rest ranged from Luttenberger's 23 years to Dufaux's 27. In other words, the new generation seemed to have arrived to challenge Indurain, who would turn 32 in a few days.

Further proof of that arrival was seemingly furnished when 26-year-old Evgeni Berzin of the Gewiss team, another bad boy of bicycle racing, pulled the overall leader's yellow jersey over his head. Berzin made Leblanc look like Mother Theresa when it came to self-interest.

Trailing Berzin in the standings were Olano, who had the same time; Rominger, seven seconds behind; and Bjarne Riis, 32, eight seconds behind. All were excellent riders in the race against the clock, which was scheduled the next day over 30.5 kilometers uphill.

If Indurain, who finished 16th and now ranked 14th, or 3:32 behind Berzin, and 3:25 behind Rominger, had a credible chance left for a sixth successive victory, he would have to start recouping in that seventh stage.

But it seemed still too early to write him off. Although the weather forecast was for more rain and cold, if a hot sun ever emerged, he might bloom. "We're not used to seeing Miguel like that," Echavarri admitted dolefully. Indeed not. The rider said later that he did not even remember crossing the finish line. When he did, he was led in an obedient stupor to a team van where he tore open a box of cookies and began pushing them into his mouth.

Zülle, who finished 15th, 3:29 behind, and ranked 11th overall, 2:30 behind, was also a fine time-trialer but had to shake off the many scrapes and bruises he received in his falls.

Three riders who had no further hope of finishing on the final one-two-three podium in Paris on July 21 were Jalabert, who finished 12:56 behind; Boardman, who lost 28:56; and Melchor Mauri, who lost the same when he was ordered to fall back and help Jalabert. Eight riders withdrew or were eliminated in the rain and cold, reducing the field to 158 of the 198 who began the race a week before.

Jalabert, who was left behind on the first climb, over the Madeleine, tried to put a positive note to the day when he told the newspaper *Journal du Dimanche*: "Getting a licking does you good. You're reminded that you're not infallible."

The man who seemed to be sitting pretty, at least for the next 24 hours, was Rominger, then the holder of the record for the hour's ride against the clock, and a climber strong enough to have won three mountain stages in the 1993 Tour, not to mention the Vuelta and the Giro.

Asked in a deluge before the start how he was feeling, Rominger replied, "We'll find out today." A man of fragile morale, he had been riding nervously the last few days, making meaningless and shortlived attacks.

The uphill time trial had been on his mind all season. In May, at the Tour DuPont, he had said, "That will change a lot. The last years, the time trial was always 50 kilometers and the specialists gained 10 minutes on the climbers. Now it's uphill."

The climbers who still might be expected to lose time included Leblanc, Luttenberger, Virenque, and Dufaux. But not Berzin, Riis, and Olano.

Stage Eight

PEOPLE HAD BEEN saying all season that Evgeni Berzin, the young Russian who startled Miguel Indurain by beating him in the Giro d'Italia in 1994, was concentrating too hard on his time-trialing skills and neglecting his climbing ability. The evidence was Berzin's victories in the races against the clock in that year's Giro and Tour of Switzerland, and his lackluster showing otherwise in both mountainous bicycle races.

Perhaps Berzin, who had turned 26 a month before the start of the Tour, was one of those prodigies who never develop further, people said, pointing to his early withdrawal in 1995 in his first Tour de France, and his lack of significant victories since the 1994 Giro.

Berzin appeared to have answered all his critics on the eighth stage by easily winning the uphill time trial and consolidating his hold on the leader's yellow jersey. With another major Alpine stage scheduled the next day, he was beginning to look like a man with climbing legs and a zest for victory.

Often criticized for his brashness and even insolence toward teammates, Berzin played his victory pianissimo. "We've only raced eight days and there are 13 still to come," he said. He also pointed out that Indurain "could be a major opponent if he regains his best condition." After faltering badly on the first Alpine stage because of what was now being explained officially, if a bit unconvincingly, as a sugar deficit, the Spaniard found himself nearly five minutes behind Berzin.

"Heaven will shine a light on all this," commented Banesto's Echavarri, fittingly on a Sunday. "Today we are in purgatory. Soon we will find out who is going up to paradise and who will be descending to hell."

Berzin finished the 30.5-kilometer stage, from Bourg St. Maurice to the resort of Val d'Isère, in 51 minutes 53 seconds. That was a speed of 35 kilometers an hour on a course that called only for power, not technique, especially into a strong headwind over the last few kilometers.

Second was Bjarne Riis, as the Dane showed the same time-trialing skills that served him so well in the Tour the previous year. He was a mere 35 seconds behind the Russian wunderkind, and third was Olano, 45 seconds behind. Rominger was fourth, 1:01 behind, in the same time as Indurain, who was fifth.

The winner led the Tour by 43 seconds over Riis, 45 seconds over Olano, and 1:08 over Rominger. Indurain was in 11th place, 4:53 behind.

"He's a specialist in the time trial and I'm not, so I'm very happy with my performance," Riis said somewhat dismissively of Berzin, his former teammate. In 1995 they both rode for Gewiss in Italy before Riis finished third in the Tour and decided, like a handful of other veterans, that he preferred not to have to work for the abrasive Russian.

"After he got third last year, maybe Riis became a little more ambitious," said Brian Holm, another Dane with the Telekom team from Germany. "Maybe he was a little surprised to get third last year. After that, he became more self-confident." Despite his disclaimer about special skills, Riis finished second to Indurain in both time trials in the previous Tour and came close — 48 seconds — to beating him in the second one.

Berzin, who started last in the individual race against the clock, was the fastest of the 157 riders at each of four checkpoints, including the finish line. As they had every day of the race, vast crowds of spectators crowded the road, which offered a spectacular view of the verdant Alps and a few distant snowy peaks.

The stage was conducted under cloudy skies in chilly and occasionally sprinkly weather. The continuing bad weather was undoing Indurain. He and his Banesto teammates were accustomed to the sun of Spain — the sun of France, too, usually during Tour time — and simply did not ride strongly in rain and cold. Unhappily for them, more of the same was forecast for the next day.

Although the defending Tour champion rode well in the time trial, he needed to begin regaining time on his opponents and to show them that he was still the boss. Fifth place did not do that in a big way. In addition, Indurain was handed a 20-second penalty for accepting soft drinks from a team car on the preceding stage as he began to weaken in the final few kilometers.

Indurain knew that he would be penalized, of course, but reckoned that he would lose more than 20 seconds without the instant jolt of energy. "He ran out of food and forgot to drink on the climbs," explained Pedro Delgado, who had won the 1988 Tour with strong help from Indurain. "In all the heavy rain this week, riders have forgotten that they need to keep drinking water all day."

That loss of power when the liver depletes its supplies of glycogen, blood sugar, is known as a *fringale* in French, the language of cycling, and in English as "the bonk."

Another rider who suffered the bonk near the finish the day before was George Hincapie. He had eaten all the food he carries in the back pockets of his jersey and drunk all the water in the bottles on his bicycle, he explained. "It was too hard to get to a team car during the climbs and descents," Hincapie continued.

"I was just empty. You're completely empty. All your power goes out gradually. Then you can barely push the pedals." He shuddered at the memory of the last five kilometers, the same distance Indurain had to ride with the bonk.

How had they felt? "Like death," Hincapie said.

Stage Nine

EVGENI BERZIN, the man without a team, should have benefited the next day when, because of overnight snow in the high Alps, intense cold and high winds, the Tour de France had to eliminate two major climbs and shorten a key mountain stage by three fourths of its scheduled length.

With the 189.5-kilometer ninth stage from Val d'Isère, France, to the resort of Sestriere, Italy, reduced to 46 kilometers, Berzin was expected to be able to keep displaying the strength that won him the overall leader's yellow jersey during the weekend.

True, his Gewiss team was especially weak in climbers able to pace Berzin and let him save his power for the final ascent. But after a few inches of snow fell on the Iseran and Galibier peaks — both rated beyond category in length, steepness, and general difficulty — and they were dropped from the stage, all the Russian had to overcome were a second-category and a first-category climb.

He could not do it. Riis, the second man in the overall standings, attacked four times on the minor climb, and held off all opposition on the bigger one, to win the stage comfortably and claim the yellow jersey. "It's strange," the Dane said prophetically, "I'm a man who likes the heat and I'm flying in the cold. Maybe I'll ride even better if it gets hot."

Riis ended his short spell in the saddle with a victory by 24 seconds over Leblanc, with Virenque third, 26 seconds behind Riis.

Rominger and Indurain finished together, fourth and fifth, 28 seconds behind Riis, as the Swiss sprinted at the very end to get his bicycle just in front of Indurain's and prove something. The winner was timed in 1 hour 10 minutes 44 seconds from the new start in Les Monetier les Bains.

Berzin, who tried to lead the chase after Riis, was exhausted halfway up the final 11-kilometer ramp. Finishing 14th, he lost 1:23 and now, in second place overall, trailed Riis by 40 seconds. Rominger was third, 53 seconds behind, and Indurain moved up to eighth, 4:38 behind.

On the final climb, Berzin got a taste of what awaited him in the Pyrenees if he reclaimed the yellow jersey. Forced to lead the chase, he had to counter alone each rider who burst past him in an attack. When the attacker saw that Berzin was on his back wheel, he refused to relay him and, by slowing, made the Russian resume the work at the head of the pack.

"It was bound to happen somewhere," the Gewiss captain said. "I don't have a team strong enough to defend the yellow jersey," which was true enough, if abundantly ungracious. Berzin was not the man to inspire a team to surpass itself nor, as events proved, was he strong enough himself to wear the yellow jersey long.

He would have faltered much earlier if the 157 riders had gone over the Iseran and the Galibier. Those peaks were eliminated by the Tour organizers in the morning when patrols reported that, although the road had been ploughed, it remained slushy and even icy in parts.

Some of those parts were on the descent from the Galibier, where gusty winds threatened to blow riders off the steep and narrow road. The temperature was viciously low, in the high 30s in the valley at the start and way below freezing on the peaks. This was July! Where was the ozone layer when you needed it?

After a week in the rain, and severe rider attrition and illness, the organizers announced that for the first time since the 1920s, a stage would be curtailed because of the weather. "Richard Virenque told me, 'But this was the stage I built my Tour around,' " said Jean-Marie Leblanc, the race's director. "But our major worry is the riders' safety and it would have been seriously compromised today." Stages in the recent past had been shortened because of labor demonstrations, usually by farmers, but once, in 1978, by the riders themselves.

The scene at the sign-in in Val d'Isère — strong winds, ear-stinging cold, rain that turned occasionally to snow, low-hanging clouds, and gloom — reminded more than one person of the resort in December, when it was annually host to the World Cup ski circuit. The decision was confirmed on the rain-whipped main street as three mountaineers brought forth lugubrious sounds from their long alpenhorns, part of the town's hospitality to a race it expected to see off in the usual heat of July.

Looking as mournful as the alpenhorns sounded was Claudio Chiappucci, the Italian climber with Carrera who won the stage to Sestriere in the 1992 Tour with a monumental breakaway in which he rode alone most of the long day and steamed into his country with a wide smile and his arms high in victory.

He hoped to repeat that triumph on the ninth stage but finished 62nd instead, 4:31 behind Riis. Chiappucci ranked 57th overall and was no longer even the leader of his team, having had to yield that role to Luttenberger, the young Austrian climber who won the Tour of Switzerland the month before and ranked sixth overall in the Tour.

Chiappucci finished second in the Tour in 1990, third the next year, and second again in 1992. He was second in the Giro d'Italia in 1991 and 1992 and third the next year. Now, with no hopes left of winning a major stage race, he looked for one-day exploits.

Gone were the days when he would attack, attack, and attack again. When opponents railed against him, he loved the attention. The man who wore the nickname El Diablo, the devil in Spanish, on his helmet never cared half so much about respect as he cared about attention. He used to wake with a song in his heart and a spring in his step. No more. These days his knees ached and the tendons in his heels were sore. He no longer coasted to the start of a stage while sitting on his handlebars.

Chiappucci was 33, old and vulnerable for a professional bicycle racer. He heard the doors closing. The next year he would change teams, he said, moving down after 12 seasons with Carrera, because he could not coexist with the younger star climber, Marco Pantani, who was injured and unavailable for the 83rd Tour.

This was the last time in the race that Chiappuci could have hoped for an exploit. But the snow, not Claudio Chiappucci, got all the attention.

Stage 10

IMAGINE THE SCENE that morning in the Jet Hotel, Via della Zecca 9 in the town of Caselle Torinese in Italy, if Miguel Indurain awoke to notice an unfamiliar light seeping through the curtains and to hear his roommate, his brother Prudencio, singing in a sweet tenor "O Sole Mio."

Big Mig opens the window, sticks his head out and sees — the sun! Great ball of fire! For the first time since the 83rd Tour started eons ago, the sky that morning was clear, the sun was blazing, and the temperature was in the 60s and climbing.

By 11:30 A.M., when the Tour left the old Fiat plant in Turin — the one where cars began to be assembled on the first floor and moved up three more floors, gaining parts, until they reached the roof complete and were driven down a ramp to a parking lot — the temperature was in the 70s, and the forecast for at least the next two days was more sun and more heat.

For Indurain, that presumed look out the window marked the real start of the Tour. The Spaniard flourishes in the sun and wilts in the cold, the rain, and even the snow in which the race had been run.

At long last, the sun. No wonder then that the Indurains arrived with the rest of the Banesto team at the sign-in for the Tour's 10th stage, 208.5 kilometers from Turin, Italy, to Gap, France, looking like two kids on the morning after school closed for the summer.

They were not alone in their jubilation. On the long road west out of town toward the Alps and a return to France after the stage into Italy, the riders were massively frisky. Attack followed attack, and never mind the brisk headwind that doomed all of them.

The last attack was by Rolf Sorensen, who was trying to prove that Riis, the man in the yellow jersey, was not the only Dane in the Tour. (In fact, there were five.) After a 25-kilometer breakaway as the race neared Gap, Sorensen could not hold off the tide of pursuers in the final straightaway.

Afterward, he sounded more than peeved that the charge after him in the final kilometer had been led by Riis, his longtime rival for Danish affection. "In Sicily, in the world championships in 1994, Riis said he lost the race because of me, because I attacked and cost him the victory," Sorensen said. "That's nonsense. I was the one who had the chance for victory. But we have this relationship that has not always been the best between us."

He was more interested, naturally, in discussing that day's stage than a race two years before. "It's confusing in your mind when you do such a great ride and everybody says 'You're the moral winner' but you don't win. It's a great disappointment. I believed until they caught me that I could do it.

"They'll need friends later," he said ominously. "When you have a team like that and you have a rider like Riis, who's capable of winning the Tour, then you let go a little bit."

He did think then that Riis, who had not been taken overly seriously yet as a possible Tour winner, could do it? "Right now, riding like he is, he's capable of winning the Tour. He's very confident and he has a good team behind him."

Proving that in the sprint finish, the winner was Erik Zabel of the Telekom team, which now held both the yellow jersey and the green jersey of the points leader. Zabel captured the green one by beating Djamolidine Abdoujaparov by half a bicycle length in the overall time of 5 hours 8 minutes 10 seconds. Andrea Ferrigato, an Italian with Roslotto, was third in the same time, which translated into 40.5 kilometers an hour. That was a rapid day's pace, considering the stage included a major climb over the Montgenèvre Pass. Credit the sunlight.

Riis remained the overall leader by 40 seconds over Berzin and 58 seconds over Rominger.

Despite the lovely day and scenic surroundings of wheat fields rippling in the headwind, a handful of riders did not survive. They included Johan Bruyneel, who was injured when he crashed off the road and into a ravine a few days earlier, and Laurent Jalabert.

The Frenchman had been considered a major contender for final victory before he vaporized on the first climb in the Alps. Losing more ground in the time trial and then in the stage shortened by snow, he was 31st, nearly 26 minutes behind, when he withdrew. "There's no room in the Tour for the sick or the weak," he said, leaving it somewhat unclear into which category he fit. "I'm going home and I'll sleep when I need sleep and train when I feel I'm up to it." Although his morale was obviously shattered, he was a prime racer and would be heard from in the next Tour and many races before that.

Indurain the elder finished lucky 13th into Gap in the same time as the winner and continued to rank eighth overall, 4:38 behind Riis.

Now that the sun was out he appeared to need only some rest. He would get that the next day when the 151 riders remaining of the 198 who started the three-week Tour got their one day off, appropriately in Gap.

If the defending champion was down, he was certainly not out, and he knew it. Although he had never had to come from so far behind his major rivals in his five victories, he remained steadfast. He knows he has to attack, he said, but attack intelligently. Although his team was weak, he had a nicely hilly stage ahead after the rest day. The Pyrenees, where he had crushed the field before, would arrive in less than a week. Finally, if he could whittle down his deficit to a minute or so, he had a long time trial to exploit on the day before the race ended.

"Have I lost the Tour?" he asked incredulously after the first time trial, repeating a question. "Are you joking? I'll tell you this: I haven't lost the Tour."

Stage 11

TEAM DEUTSCHE TELEKOM called a news conference on the rest day to flaunt its, and the Tour de France's, leader, Bjarne Riis, plus its sprinter, Erik Zabel, the wearer of the green points jersey, and its *wunderkind*, Jan Ullrich, who was seventh in the competition for the polka-dot jersey of the best climber

Those were all the special jerseys in the race. If there still had been a white one for the best rider under the age of 25, Ullrich, 22, would have been wearing it.

Because Telekom's domination was so complete, little was heard about the major challengers to Riis on stage 11 other than details about a high-speed crash by Rominger — another one for the Swiss rider, the third-ranked rider among the 146 remaining. Although he was reported to have cut and bruised his right leg, his wounds were described as superficial.

"This bad luck is starting to get to me," the rider complained. "I had two wheel changes, a big scare at the feed when a wheel broke and I nearly fell off. Then I crashed coming down the last descent. It's a bit much."

A spokesman for his Mapei team said that more would be known about Rominger's condition after a night's sleep and the expected stiffening of his leg. What was worrisome, the spokesman added, was that the rider's right knee was already troubling him before the crash left it scraped.

Otherwise, as the Tour completed its 202-kilometer spin from Gap over six moderate climbs to Valence, the favorites spent the day regarding each other and letting a long breakaway of eight low-ranked riders battle for the victory. Nobody else was in the mood to challenge Telekom.

If the team was so respected, why was it lodged for the day off in the deep boondocks — take the two-lane blacktop northeast out of Gap, keep going past fields strewn with bales of hay, hang a left at the herd of cows crossing the road and a right at the pine tree blazed with a big X — instead of in the city with most of the rest of the big boys?

The accommodations were the type that the Tour organizers usually reserve for second-rank teams from Spain. Perhaps when the hotel list was drawn up the previous fall, nobody thought Telekom would be worthy of anything better.

Not so, said the hotel's proprietor. He boasted that three previous Tour winners — Greg LeMond, Pedro Delgado, and Miguel Indurain — had stayed under his roof the years that they triumphed.

Telekom would go downtown in the next Tour. This was not the 1995 team.

"We didn't have a real leader last year," explained Walter Godefroot, the team's Belgian director. The year before, without Riis at the helm, Telekom was admitted to the Tour only as a mixed entry with the equally undistinguished ZG team from Italy. The blend lived up to expectations. "Also we didn't have the maturity and stability that we have this year," Godefroot added.

Or, as Sorensen said of Telekom, "When you're on the edge, you tend to perform better. Riis has brought the team up to the edge."

Riis, then 32, continued to do that on the 11th stage as he retained his 40-second lead over Berzin. Both of them, and all other favorites, including Rominger, finished 2 minutes 51 seconds behind the winner of the stage, Chepe Gonzalez, a Colombian with the Kelme team who started the day in 117th place. Taking off in the final straightaway, Gonzalez coasted home a second ahead of Manuel Fernandez Gines, a Spaniard with Mapei, and rose to 107th place overall, more than 1 hour 13 seconds behind Riis. The diminutive Gonzalez was timed in 5 hours 9 minutes 12 seconds, a speed of 39 kilometers an hour.

Conducted mainly in sunshine over Alpine foothills, the stage was watched by large crowds, including a few hundred disgruntled farmers who tried to interrupt proceedings in the cause of lower taxes, and a few dozen riot policemen who stood nearby to tamp down the tempers of the sons of the soil.

Riis was one of them himself, a reserved fellow who grew up in the Danish countryside, spent his first seven seasons in the sport as a worker for team leaders and only began to emerge in 1993, when he finished fifth in the Tour as a member of the Ariostea team. With Gewiss the previous year he finished third and jumped at the chance to lead a team.

"It's good, it's different," he said about his new role before he began heading for the yellow jersey in the Alps.

During his years of servitude with the Roland, Lucas, Toshiba, Super U and Castorama teams, where he carried bottles of water, chased down breakaways, and rode tempo for his leader, had he ever thought that he would become a leader?

"No, you don't think about that," he replied. "Now, in this position, you think about it."

He was thinking about more than that. At his news conference, he switched from French to Italian to sort of Spanish — he also speaks English and, of course, Danish and German — to discuss his chances of victory.

"Paris," he said with a big smile, "it's still so far away." But, he added, "My position is ideal. I'm riding well and the team is very strong. I've never had such good form as I have now."

His teammate and fellow Dane, Brian Holm, agreed with that analysis. "He thinks he can win this race," Holm said. "He seems stronger than he was last year — he's making more results. After he got third last year, maybe he became a little more ambitious. Maybe he was a little surprised to get third last year.

"After that, he became more self-confident. Now he believes maybe he can win. Maybe he believes that." While those were a lot of "maybes," this was Holm speaking. Riis did not use the word.

He sat in the hotel's dining room under mounted heads of deer and rams presumably shot in the hills outside Gap. Locals peered in the windows, and in the nearby lobby a phone rang. Riis spoke without a microphone and the room resounded with appeals of "sh" from reporters trying to catch his words as he switched languages.

"I think I'm very capable of winning," he decided. "I think I'm the strongest rider right now." Indurain? "It depends on how he progresses. I don't think there will be much change in the general classification in the next few stages. That will happen probably at Hautacam." Rominger? "Mapei is a strong team, and Rominger is the only leader now. But Olano could step up."

Riis? "I think I'm very capable of winning," he repeated. "But I can't afford to be sick or weak one day as Miguel was."

Stage 12

THEY ALL LAUGHED when Daisuke Imanaka sat down to ride the Tour de France but, in the words of the old song, "Ha, ha, ha, ho, ho, ho, who has the last laugh now?"

Imanaka, that's who. Imanaka, the survivor.

The field of 198 riders who started the race dwindled to 145 after the 143.5-kilometer 12th stage from Valence over five minor and pretty climbs to the small city of Le Puy en Velay. Long gone from the pack were such celestial names as Johan Bruyneel, the leader of the Rabobank team; Mario Cipollini, the flamboyant sprinter; Stéphane Heulot, who wore the leader's yellow jersey for a few days; Lance Armstrong, the former world road-race champion; and Laurent Jalabert, the world's No. 1 rider in computerized standings.

Still in the race, still showing up each day to sign in, still crossing every finish line was Imanaka, then 33, a Japanese whose results in his three professional seasons with the Polti team from Italy ranked him 719th globally. In this Tour, his first, he was in 144th place, second from last, more than two hours behind the leader.

Imanaka was unable to revise his position despite a strong finish in 35th place in the 12th stage, which was won in a sprint by Pascal Richard, a Swiss with MG, by a couple of bicycle lengths over Jesper Skibby, a Dane with TVM. Mirco Gualdi, an Italian with Polti, was third.

Skibby, who, like Sorensen a few days before, wanted to show the huge crowd of spectators that Riis was not the sole rider from Denmark in the race, turned out to be just a semi-great Dane once Richard unleashed his power and won so handily that he coasted the last 10 meters. "The Tour lasts 21 days and riders like me sometimes ask ourselves if it's worth all that effort for one stage victory," Richard said. "Today, I feel that it is."

He was timed in 3 hours 29 minutes 19 seconds, an average speed of 41 kilometers an hour over the hills of the Massif Central, which were whipped by the mistral, a north wind, especially on the summits.

Once again the leaders, including the battered Rominger, watched each other and were content to let a nine-man breakaway of riders low in the overall standings win by a big margin. Although the main pack finished 15:14 behind the nine, Richard managed to rise only from 43rd place to 31st, nearly 30 minutes down in total elapsed time.

To Imanaka, such a height in the standings would probably cause a nose bleed.

"I'm a little bit tired," the Japanese said before the pack set off. But there he was, continuing as a Tour de France rider. He grinned. Imanaka grins and laughs a lot.

He was not surprised by his survival, he said. "Last year I rode in the Giro d'Italia and I raced hard in every stage and almost made it to the end." He withdrew in the mountainous 14th of 20 stages in the Giro.

"The Tour de France is harder," he continued. "Most of my races have been 120 or 150 kilometers, not this long." Eight of the Tour's first 11 stages had been at least 199 kilometers long and the entire race would cover 3,900 kilometers.

The Alps were especially difficult, he said. "Very high, very hard." The Tour was passing through rolling terrain in the south of France at that moment and would enter the Pyrenees mountains in a few days. When this was pointed out, Imanaka shuddered, then laughed.

Aside from Mount Fuji, he said, he was not familiar with mountains before he moved to Italy in 1994, settling in Bergamo and joining the Polti team. "After this, I'd like to try to go up Mount Fuji," he said.

A native of Hiroshima who now lived in Osaka, he was the first Japanese professional in the Tour, whose organizers searched their records and found that a Japanese amateur competed in the 1920s, when riders could drop in for a daily stage or two.

To general surprise, Imanaka had lasted 12 stages already. The *directeur sportif* of his team, Gianluigi Stanga, must have been the most surprised of all. "He's really sponsored by Shimano, which furnishes components for our bicycles," Stanga had explained coldly. "After he rode the Giro, he dreamed of doing the Tour. Since nobody else jumped out at me as a choice" for the last spot on the nine-man team, "I gave him this present. Anyway, it's very difficult to get all your riders to Paris."

But see, he held. Polti had lost two other riders while Imanaka continued to head for Paris. Moreover, he had gained a minor reputation for his ability to descend, if not climb, mountains at high speed.

It was no secret that he was testing new Shimano equipment on his bicycle during the Tour and reporting back often to company headquarters in Japan. After college, Imanaka became one of Japan's few road racers and then began working for Shimano in research and development.

The giant supplier, which makes almost everything for a bicycle except rims and spokes, was working on a nine-speed cassette, instead of the usual eight-speed, and Imanaka was giving the system a road test in the Tour.

"No mechanical problems," he said. "This is very nice equipment. It's working well."

Like his legs?

Imanaka broke up. "My legs," he said as he roared with laughter. "Oh, my legs," he said, convulsed by the last laugh.

Stage 13

MIGUEL INDURAIN and his Banesto teammates finally went on the attack, raising an already high speed at the start of the final three climbs in the 13th stage in an effort to move the defending champion up in the standings. To a point, the ambush worked, but only to a point.

Indurain, who started the day in eighth place overall, 4 minutes 38 seconds behind the leader, did gain a bit of time over a few riders ahead of him. He also lost a bit to a few. He failed, however, to change the gap with Riis, who continued to ride like a man determined to win the Tour. The Dane used his Telekom teammates skillfully, even dropping back to wait for one, Jan Ullrich, who faltered on a climb and then returned with Riis's assistance to work hard for his leader.

Indurain had no such help available. His weaker team spent itself at the start of the climb, so he stayed on Riis's back wheel but could not get around and away from the man in the yellow jersey.

For the Spaniard, the day was a wash: Although he showed that he had recovered his strength after that disastrous day in the Alps, he also learned that Riis did not appear ready to bend, let alone break.

Indurain finished the 177-kilometer slog from Le Puy en Velay through the Massif Central to the resort of Superbesse in his familiar eighth place. His opportunities to take back a big part of his deficit and win a sixth successive Tour seemed to be ebbing.

The stage was won by Sorensen, who was not a contender in the Tour but would be in the road race at the Olympic Games in Atlanta, his main goal. Sorensen broke away with 13 other low-ranked riders long before the three final climbs, and had enough juice left in the sprint to hold off one of his companions, Orlando Rodrigues, a Portuguese with Banesto, and two of the fast-closing chase group of favorites, Virenque of Festina and Leblanc of Polti.

The winner was timed in 4 hours 3 minutes 56 seconds, a rapid 43.5 kilometers an hour in occasionally cloudy weather and not enough wind to stir the grass in the endless cattle pastures en route. Rodrigues and Virenque had the same time and Leblanc two seconds more.

In sixth place for the stage, Indurain led in most of the other contenders 23 seconds behind Sorensen. The major losers of time among the favorites were Rominger and Berzin, both of whom finished 18 seconds behind the Indurain-Riis group.

Overall, Riis now led Olano by 56 seconds. The Spaniard started the day in fourth place by the same difference in total elapsed time. Dropping down a notch each were Berzin, now third, 1:08 behind, and Rominger, now fourth, 1:21 behind.

Bernard Hinault, who won the Tour five times and now served as one of its public relations men, was willing — eager, actually — to offer his usual advice: Attack. He had been saying that for more than a week, but nobody seemed to be listening.

"Olano must attack," the Badger told a newspaper, the *Journal du Dimanche*. "Then Riis must go after him and Rominger will be waiting to attack again when Riis is tired." Of Rominger, Hinault added, "I wonder where he will attack. He is losing chances day after day." His morale wobbling, his knee throbbing, the Swiss did not heed the advice, if he read it. "After I fell the other day, I got back to the hotel thinking that this Tour isn't for me, that it's too difficult," Rominger told a Spanish reporter. "A question was going around in my head: 'What am I doing here?' " Hinault, who always believed that the best defense was a strong offense, would not have appreciated that attitude.

With the Pyrenees ahead, the times between the top five leaders would have been differences of a nanosecond if Riis had not been riding so well and so confidently. His teammate Holm reported that when Riis was trailing some of the other favorites by 25 seconds during the previous day's stage, Telekom riders asked him if they should tow him up to the leaders.

"Don't worry about it," Holm quoted Riis as having said. "I can catch them whenever I want to." A few minutes later he did just that, and effortlessly, Holm said.

The 13th stage was again watched by an enormous number of fans, especially on the last climbs, narrowing the small road to Superbesse even further. It was an ideal place for an ambush since a rider trapped at the rear of the 25-kilometer climb would have found it nearly impossible to move through the cramped 143-man pack and respond to an attack at the front.

The Banesto team had its tactics right but was slowed in executing them when Indurain had a flat tire early in the ascent. He quickly took a rear wheel from a teammate's bicycle and his Banestos resumed their fast pace, hoping to open a gap between the defending champion and his rivals.

After a while, the team began to lag and, with Rodrigues far ahead in the breakaway and of no immediate assistance, it was up to Indurain alone. While he rode forcefully, Riis matched him stroke for stroke. The Dane was beginning to look untouchable.

Stage 14

HERE IT WAS BASTILLE DAY, the French national holiday, the day on which almost every French rider would give his rear wheel for a victory in the Tour de France.

And the winner of the 14th of 21 stages was — Djamolidine Abdoujaparov, the Uzbek. That's Uzbek as in a native of Uzbekistan, about two months' journey eastbound by bicycle from France. He lives in Italy, where he races for the Refin team.

Abdoujaparov, the victor of eight Tour sprints over the years, and twice the winner of the green points jersey, culminated a longish breakaway with four companions — two of them French — by leaving them in his dust (*la poussière*) with two kilometers sharply uphill to go. He had enough power (*la force*) to win by seven seconds over Mirco Gualdi, an (*nom de Dieu*) Italian with the Polti team.

So what if, in the patois, Abdoujaparov was able to *mettre des batons dans les roues* (put some sticks in the French wheels)? Nine seconds back, in third place, was Laurent Madouas. Seven further seconds behind in fourth place was Didier Rous, a Frenchman with Gan. Let the dancing in the streets resume.

Abdou was timed in 4 hours 6 minutes 29 seconds as he blew whatever chance he had for the Legion d'Honneur. In a stage run in sunny heat in the high 80s and under a sky of marshmallow clouds, his speed averaged better than 45 kilometers an hour.

That rapid pace resulted in the elimination of three riders, the Japanese Daisuke Imanaka among them, for finishing outside the time limit. Imanaka finished last, 41:23 behind. Along with three riders who quit, the eliminations reduced the field to 137 among the 198 who started.

George Hincapie also finished outside the limit but was spared because he crashed heavily on a descent and needed time to be patched up before he could resume riding. He withdrew from the Tour the next morning.

Abdoujaparov's high speed was also more than the leaders of the Tour felt like following. They arrived nearly five minutes behind the Tashkent Terror, as Abdou is known for his habit of putting his head down in sprints and weaving hither and yon among his rivals, just the way he did as a boy in camel races back home.

Riis remained in the yellow jersey, 56 seconds ahead of Olano and 1:14 ahead of Berzin. Moving up to 12th place overall was another member of the breakaway, Bo Hamburger, a Dane with TVM, who finished fifth. He started the day in 16th place, 11 minutes down, and jumped to 12th, 6:38 behind.

Indurain remained in eighth place, 4:38 behind and came mighty close to falling, like the Bastille, on this day. He was trapped with 15 kilometers gone and the pack on a climb of 7 kilometers at a grade of 5.7 percent up to the Croix Morand pass. Alone among the leaders, Indurain and Rominger were in the rear of the caravan.

As Riis went over the top, he accelerated. Followed swiftly by teammates and other major riders, the man in the yellow jersey was suddenly 25 seconds ahead of Indurain and Rominger. Behind them, Indurain and five of his Banesto teammates were leading a losing chase.

The lead mounted from Kilometer 21.5, the site of the attack, to 42 seconds by Kilometer 43 and a full minute shortly afterward. Only when the ONCE and Kelme teams, also from Spain, joined the weak Banestos at the front did the lead begin coming down.

By Kilometer 60, everybody was back together again, the trap unsprung. It was not like Indurain to be caught at the rear when all his rivals were at the front and it was another sign that his accustomed luck, like his leg strength, was not what it had been the last five years.

Similarly, the attack by Riis, which matched a basically fruitless one by Indurain the day before, showed that he was either very strong or extremely confident. Perhaps it even showed both.

More would be known once the Tour entered the Pyrenees in two days, Indurain's 32d birthday. Ominously, among the four riders who have won the Tour a record five times — Jacques Anquetil, Eddy Merckx, Bernard Hinault and Indurain — only the Spaniard had been able to record a victory after his 31st birthday. Indurain could celebrate the big day with an ascension of the fearsome Hautacam peak, followed the next day by a long, mountainous journey from France to Pamplona, Spain, just outside the village where he grew up.

At that point, his chances were not extinct. Banesto team officials made public a letter from Charly Gaul, the Tour winner by 3:10 in 1958, in which the Luxembourg veteran said: "When I won the Tour, I was 15 minutes behind with three days to go. In just one stage, I put 20 minutes into Anquetil and half an hour into Bahamontes. Nothing is lost. Good luck."

Once peace was restored after the Riis attack, the pack allowed a series of attacks by low-ranked riders, many of them Frenchmen who remembered the acclaim that Vincent Barteau gained in 1992, when he won solo in Marseille on Bastille Day, and that Laurent Jalabert gained in 1995 when he won solo into Mende on the same holiday.

Usually joined immediately by Italian riders, the Frenchmen did their best to escape over roads awash in gravel loosened by melting tar. François Simon, Laurent Brochard, Thierry Bourgignon, Gilles Talmant, Laurent Roux — one after another they tried and were thwarted. Bastille Day was Abdou's holiday.

But, as François Lemarchand, a French rider with Gan, said before the stage, "People make too much about a French rider winning on Bastille Day. A victory on July 15 is just as wonderful as one on July 14."

Stage 15

WHEN HE GREETED his fan club, Laurent Roux would have preferred to be alone — off, say, on a huge breakaway in the Tour de France or, even better, a huge and victorious breakaway. Then, like some champions of old, he could have gotten off his bicycle, eaten an ice cream, and signed autographs before resuming his triumphant ride.

Instead, Roux was simply another face in the pack when it whizzed past an open-air celebration by his supporters that recalled the days when the bicycle race was somewhat closer to the people than modern corporate practices allow.

Roux did his best to make the rendezvous. An hour earlier, he joined a five-man counterattack, which might have gone somewhere and thrilled his fans, but it was quickly swallowed by the pack. After that, he could do no more than wave at Kilometer 117 of the 15th stage, which covered 176 kilometers of engagingly rolling country from Brive la Gaillarde to Villeneuve-sur-Lot in the southwest.

He missed a swell time, complete with free *foie gras* and the wine of Cahors, two products of the region, as is Roux. In what obviously served the rest of the year as a cow pasture, a seven- person band, including three on accordion, played such tunes as "Go Laurent, He Can Win" and "To the Champs-Elysées, Perhaps He Can Win."

What was with the "perhaps?" That was no way for a fan club to think. All together now, every last one of the 262 members of the Association of the Supporters of Laurent Roux: When the Tour ended in Paris, he was a cinch to win.

Then, but not this day. Massimo Podenzana, whose fan club, if any, was based in his native Italy, glided across the finish line, the winner by 37 seconds after he shed his companions in another long breakaway by low-ranked riders. Second to the Carrera rider was Giuseppe Guerini, an Italian with Polti, and third in the six-man avant garde was Peter Van Petegem, a Belgian with TVM, 50 seconds behind.

Podenzana, twice the champion of Italy, completed the stage in 3 hours 54 minutes 52 seconds, a stunning average of 44.9 kilometers an hour considering the heavy heat, which reached 92 degrees Fahrenheit. Where were the snows of yesterweek?

Riis continued comfortably in the overall lead as all the contenders finished 5:38 behind, content for a third day to watch each other and await the Pyrenees, where battle would be joined at the highest level.

That was not yet Roux's. Then 23 years old and in his third year as a professional, he ranked a creditable 40th among the 135 riders remaining. Showing strong spirit, Roux had often gone on the attack in the Tour for his TVM team, which is based in the Netherlands. He joined TVM after his first employer, Castorama in France, folded at the end of 1995.

The picture postcard that his fan club was selling for five francs ($1) noted that he had twice been selected to represent France in the world championships, that he won a race in Picardy and finished second in the Classique des Alpes in 1994 and won a stage and finished third overall in the esteemed Tour de l'Avenir in 1995. In 1996, he had won a stage in the Route du Sud and finished second in the French championship road race.

He had a nice smile, looked good in his team jersey and wore a discreet ring in his left ear. What more could a fan club ask for?

So the worktables in the press room after the 14th stage into Tulle were covered with invitations for the 1,000 reporters who travel with the race to attend the shindig in his honor. "Thanks in advance for coming by," the bottom of the paper read. "Friendship and thanks for your encouragement," Roux wrote underneath.

The food, the wine, the conversations with the people who line the sides of the Tour's many roads were all a throwback to the time, about a decade ago, when such encounters were common. Let the race go through the village of Renazé in the Mayenne, for example, and the members of the Madiot Brother's Club — the punctuation was theirs — always set up trestle tables bearing food and drink in honor of Marc and Yvon Madiot, two fine French riders. Let the race pass through a town in the Dordogne or the Auvergne where a former champion lived and the festivities were repeated.

Everybody, from reporters to team mechanics to the drivers of the race's hundreds of cars, was welcome to enjoy a quick plate of cold cuts, a slice of bread, a bit of gossip. Then, with the race approaching, back into the cars and on down the road.

Nowadays the practice was discouraged by the Tour's organizers. Probably there were insurance risks and possibly there was a feeling that these meals were not quite as chic an image as the race wanted to present. Like the homely broom that used to serve as a mast on the bus, known as the broom wagon, that sweeps up riders who have quit the race, the fans' lunches have disappeared.

Instead, at each stage's start there is the official Village Départ, surrounded by high fences and guarded by officials who check the credentials of anybody who tries to enter and rub elbows with riders and journalists. Invitations are issued to businessmen, politicians, and other people who might help the Tour or any of the teams represented. The man in the street, the fan who wants an autograph or a glimpse of his favorite rider? He stands outside, behind barricades.

So the party for Roux was a rare one indeed, a reminder of less formal times when the cars filling the road behind a breakaway belonged to the press and teams, not to the Tour itself and its many sponsors. The signs at the cow pasture said, "Vive Laurent Roux." Second the motion and, just as good, "Vive the Laurent Roux Fan Club."

Stage 16

BJARNE RIIS did it at Lourdes-Hautacam and Miguel Indurain didn't. Riis climbed magnificently, riding away from the field as the Tour reached the Pyrenees and the awaited showdown among the contenders. The Dane easily won the 16th stage by leaving everybody far behind halfway up the 13.5-kilometer climb to the desolate and windswept Hautacam peak.

Indurain faltered badly when Riis attacked for a fourth time on the ascent. The Spaniard began to labor, fell behind the group of riders he accompanied, and struggled alone toward the top. This was a pitiable way to spend his 32nd birthday.

"I tried to follow three times, and the fourth time I gave up," Indurain reported. "Riis was very strong. I couldn't follow anyone, not Rominger, not Olano. Maybe if they had slowed a bit I would have been able to recover. But the climb got tougher and tougher while I felt they were going faster and faster. The gap with Riis can't be closed unless he explodes. The day when you lose to the favorite is the day you lose the Tour."

When Riis crossed the finish line with his arms raised and one finger on each hand up to signify his ranking as No. 1, nobody could argue. Although the long stage to Pamplona lay a day ahead, he was evidently unbeatable.

"I have a feeling that the Hautacam was made for me," Riis said a few days before, displaying the confidence that had marked his rise from fifth place in the 1993 Tour to third place in 1995 and now the yellow jersey. How right he was. The Telekom leader won by 49 seconds over Virenque and his Festina teammate, Laurent Dufaux. Indurain finished 2 minutes 28 seconds behind, in 12th place.

More important, the Dane opened some breathing room over his major rivals. He started the day 56 seconds up on the second-place Olano, who now trailed in second by 2:42. Rominger, still third, fell to 2:54 behind. Indurain dropped to 10th place, an unmanageable 7:06 behind. The other major fall of the day was suffered by Berzin, who declined from third place to sixth, 4:07 behind.

"I think that three minutes, if I can hold that lead until the time trial, will be enough for me to win the Tour," the man in the yellow jersey said afterward, stretching his margin a bit.

He finished the stage in 4 hours 56 minutes 16 seconds, an average of 40 kilometers an hour. On the Hautacam itself, he rode the 13.5 kilometers under a hot sun in 34 minutes, or 90 seconds faster than Indurain and Luc Leblanc did in a more comfortable drizzle two years earlier when they dueled for victory — it went to the Frenchman — far ahead of the pack.

Riis triumphed so easily that the only trouble he had after he broke away alone was when he swerved too closely to a spectator's car parked along the road to the top. Hundreds of thousands of fans, many of them Spaniards who crossed the nearby border, watched the race in hot and sunny weather.

Depending on where they stood along the narrow road, the fans saw the contenders bunched after some early attacks low on the climb. Jan Ullrich was leading his captain plus Indurain and a dozen others ahead of the pack when Riis suddenly moved to the right and slid back along the line of riders.

It looked like a moment of weakness, but it wasn't. "I was just checking on peoples' condition," Riis explained later. "I dropped back down the group to see how the others looked. They were having trouble following, so I thought, 'It's now or never, you must win the Tour now'." He shot to the front and attacked.

Indurain stayed with him. When Riis accelerated again and again, that was the end of Indurain and everybody else.

The 199-kilometer stage was conducted over mainly flat country until it reached the wall of the Hautacam, high above the pilgrims' city of Lourdes and its grotto. The stage began in Agen, the prune capital of the universe, where an unwary visitor could sample such hospitality as prune juice, prunes in their pure state, prunes stuffed with prunes and, treacherously, prunes concealed in chocolates.

Shortly after the 134 riders departed, hanging a right where a statue of the 19th-century poet Jacques Jasmin pointed at a house shuttered against the blazing sun, a three-man attack was allowed to take off after a couple of others had been foiled.

Leading the threesome was Laurent Roux, a native of the Lot region where the stage began. The day before he could not break away to salute his fan club but on this stage he was given free rein, along with Pascal Richard and Mariano Piccoli.

Past fields of sunflowers rolling uphill to the horizon they flew, past tidy villages of cream-colored houses with red tiled roofs. The fugitives' lead exceeded seven minutes at Kilometer 63, which suited the overall leaders' strategy: Nobody could counterattack riders so far ahead, and the stage could continue bunched until the breakaway was reeled in by the beginning of the Hautacam, where the real race began.

Roux did his best to thwart this grand design. Looking determined as he took his turns at the front of the break, he began leaving his companions behind by Kilometer 150, where a sharp left turn offered the first view of the distant smudges that were the Pyrenees. His lead of four minutes began diminishing, however, and was barely above three when he rode by fields of grazing cows draped in blankets colored yellow or white with red polka dots in imitation of the jerseys of the Tour's leader and king of the mountains.

By the Hautacam, his lead was in seconds and he was cooked. Roux managed to climb ahead of the charging pack for a kilometer or so before he yielded, finishing 51st, 10:37 behind.

Once Roux was gone, the center of attraction became Indurain until he cracked, and then Riis, all the way to the top only Riis.

Stage 17

E L REY MIGUEL INDURAIN V came home a hero in the Tour. After five consecutive victories in the race, the king would not soon be changing the number after his name to VI — Bjarne Riis had won the race, barring accident or illness before the finish. But that seemed to matter not at all to hundreds of thousands of Indurain's fans in Pamplona, the finish, and a similar number along the route from France into Spain.

"Miguel, Miguel, Miguel," thousands chanted as he rode through Villava, the town where he grew up, and then just down the road into Pamplona. In the grandstands they rose and applauded him. Eight minutes behind in the stage, Indurain rode the final two kilometers through a corridor of drumming as his fellow Spaniards beat rhythmically on aluminum barriers and screamed his name.

Finally, looking drawn, he mounted the platform that is usually reserved for the day's winner and the overall leaders in three categories: the top climber, the points leader, and the man in the yellow jersey, the No. 1. That was the number Indurain wore in this Tour after his victory the year before. His jersey was not the leaders' white with polka dots, green, or yellow, however. He wore simply the white, red, and blue colors of his Banesto team for the first time this late in the Tour since 1990.

Indurain tried to manage a smile for his adoring crowd. Then Riis, who finished second in the mountainous 17th stage and now led by nearly four minutes, presented his bouquet to Indurain and raised the Spaniard's arm. Indurain waved, threw the flowers out into the horde, and climbed slowly down the stairs and off the victors' platform.

Riis stayed on. The Dane led a long breakaway in the Pyrenees by eight riders that exploded the standings and left him invulnerable at the top. "I've won, but you mustn't forget that Miguel Indurain is still a great champion," he told the crowd. "If I couldn't have won, I would have liked Miguel Indurain to have won."

With four of 21 stages to go, Riis was 3 minutes 59 seconds ahead of his teammate Ullrich in second place and 4:25 ahead of Virenque. Ullrich would not attack his leader, of course, and Virenque was so thrilled at the prospect of becoming the first Frenchman since 1989 to stand on the Tour's final one-two-three victory podium that he would assuredly do nothing to incite retribution.

In fourth place, 5:52 behind, was the winner of the long and demanding stage into Pamplona, Laurent Dufaux. In a two-man sprint at the end of the 262-kilometer grind over five major mountains, the Swiss passed Riis with a few meters to go.

Twenty seconds behind them, in order, were Virenque, Ullrich, Luc Leblanc, Piotr Ugrumov, Fernando Escartin of Spain, riding for Kelme, and Peter Luttenberger. Those were the men of the breakaway that started on the fourth climb, up to the Soudet Pass, 18 kilometers of ascent on a grade of 6.3 percent, and those were the eight who now led the overall standings.

Indurain was in 11th place, 15:36 behind, the lowest he had been in the Tour in this decade. He must have been wondering what had happened to his legs. They failed him again for the second day in the Pyrenees, just as they had in the Alps. The man who had constructed his Tour victories out of overwhelming triumphs in long time trials and the ability to stay with the best climbers in the mountains was simply not up to the job in this Tour.

On the Soudet climb, when riders began taking water bottles from fans to stave off the fiery sun, Indurain fell behind halfway up. He was not alone. Olano and Rominger, in second and third place overall when the stage began in the French town of Argelès-Gazost, were among those who also faltered. They now ranked ninth and tenth.

At the front, Riis with his teammates and Virenque with his pressed their attack. On the fifth and final major climb, 14.8 kilometers up to the Port de Larrau, the gap increased. No wonder: the average grade was 7.7 percent with portions up to a numbingly steep 11 percent. From two minutes, the time between the Riis group and the Indurain group grew to three. Riis himself broke the spirit of the chasing group when, on the dinky final climb up the 5-kilometer-long Alta de Garralda hill, he went to the front and pushed so hard that the margin widened to four minutes. When they heard that news, the chasers lost hope.

Over the final 107 kilometers of rolling descent to Pamplona, the margin rose to five, six, seven, and then 8 minutes 30 seconds at the line. Dufaux took 7 hours 7 minutes 8 seconds for his journey, an average of 36.8 kilometers an hour in a stage that saw the field reduced by five riders to 129.

Riding in a hopeless chase with about a dozen others, Indurain might have been encouraged by the spectators, both in France and then in Spain and his native Navarre Province when the race passed over the Port de Larrau. Support was everywhere. "*Aupá Indurain,*" (Hop, or go, Indurain) read the banners. Dozens of villages posted signs with their names linked with his. Thousands of fans waved cardboard busts of him in the yellow jersey that a newspaper had distributed.

In a Dutch newspaper that morning, Riis was quoted as having said, "I would like Indurain to win tomorrow because we are going past his home, but it won't be easy for him." So did many other people hope.

If the Tour was over for Indurain, there would be another Tour in a year and at least one fan was already looking ahead to it. A sign somewhere in the sweltering approach to Pamplona told the champion: "Miguel, Super 1997."

Stage 18

RELIEF WAS IN SIGHT for Frankie Andreu, so close that he could measure it: 437.5 more kilometers, roughly 270 more miles, three more days and he would have finished his fifth Tour de France in five attempts.

"I'm pretty confident I'll make it now," he said before the start of the 18th stage. "I really had doubts that first week whether I would make it, so I'm happy." He crashed and injured his left leg and right ankle on the first stage in the Netherlands, and then struggled through more than a week of rain and heavy wind, having to push a big gear.

"Every year you say, 'Never again, it's so hard and so miserable,' and then when the Tour rolls around again, you start getting motivated and you find yourself back here," he continued. "But it's not fun."

For Andreu, then 29, the last few days especially had not been fun. Forget about the stage into Pamplona, where he finished 70th, 33 minutes behind. Forget about the stage the next day, when he had to push his weary legs over 154.5 kilometers from that Spanish city to Hendaye, France, on the Atlantic.

The last few days had been draining because Andreu had been Motorola's point man in memorial observances for Fabio Casartelli, the young rider who died a year before, following a crash on a descent in the Pyrenees in which his skull was fractured.

On the anniversary, Andreu was the riders' representative at a small service at the monument to Casartelli at the spot where he crashed and hit a cement stanchion. Two days later, as the only member of the team still in the Tour who rode the previous year with the 24-year-old Italian, Andreu received a plaque and a bouquet from the leading rider under the age of 25, a competition that has been named for Casartelli.

"I think about him every single day I get on the bike," Andreu said afterward. "When I get on the bike, I'm doing my passion, my love for cycling, which is just what he was doing. I feel fortunate, and every day I miss him."

Then it was time to race, and Andreu joined the pack for the trip over five climbs to Hendaye. The 129 weary riders moved slowly at the start — a paltry speed of 26 kilometers during the first hour — before 14 found the energy to mount or join a long breakaway. At the finish, with ocean breezes disguising a torrid temperature, Bart Voskamp, a Dutchman with TVM, had enough zip left to hold off Christian Henn, the German national champion, who rode for Telekom. Voskamp was timed in 4 hours 11 minutes 2 seconds, two seconds ahead of his pursuer and an average of 37 kph.

Andreu and the rest of the pack except for the 14 escapees finished 16:56 behind. The American was in 111th place overall, a meaningless statistic since he was the model support rider, a man who worked to protect his leader, not his own interests.

The man in the yellow jersey, Riis, was untroubled during the stage, as he no doubt would be all the way to Paris. The Dane had highly impressed Andreu — and everybody else — throughout. "Everytime I saw him, he was looking good, looking comfortable, very strong," the American said. "He came here after finishing third last year and everybody was wondering, 'How can he do it?' and how Miguel was going to be, but on those days that were critical, Riis made sure everybody knew he was the strongest. He almost showed off his strength, put everybody in their place.

"He definitely deserved to win the Tour. He's the strongest guy here. He rode great last year and you could see the steps coming up" after he finished fifth in 1993. "But I think the big surprise is how much he dominated everybody else. All the other big guys blew."

The Motorola rider preferred to look not back but ahead, to Paris. For Andreu, that day would mean "a lot of personal satisfaction."

"If I start something, I'm committed to it, not only for myself but for the team. It's the Tour de France. A lot of people don't find any prestige in finishing it, but I do. I agree that it's more important to race the Tour than ride it just to be able to finish. I've been trying to race it and finish too."

Like everybody else on the Motorola team, Andreu was uncertain about his future since the sponsor was bowing out. "Whatever happens, I want to keep racing in Europe," he said. "I feel every year I'm getting stronger, although the problem is that every year the pack is getting stronger too. I keep being a little bit behind, but I'm going in the right direction. I think I can still do some damage in Europe.

"If this team can't stay together, then I have to move on. This sport is a business. So I've been talking to other teams. But I'm holding off as long as I can."

He did not anticipate major difficulties in finding another employer. Andreu was known as a selfless rider and a strong one — that spring he won the Olympic Trials in the United States and a place on the five-man team for the Olympic road race.

"I know what my job is there," he said. "To work for Lance Armstrong. I have no problem with that. That's one of the things that's kept me on this team: being realistic about what my job is. I know I'm not a champion, I know I'm not going to win the classics or the World Cup overall.

"I think I make the most of my abilities. Lance is in a class of his own. So I go to Atlanta and work for him because he has the best chance of doing something. I know that. I know what my role is and I give 100 percent and that's the best I can ask for. Sure I would love to win more but it doesn't come so easy. At all."

Stage 19

KAMIKAZE FIRST CLASS Eros Poli wanted to deny the report that he had grounded himself. Yes, he did say after the stage to Pamplona, with its five major climbs and 262 kilometers, that henceforth his ambitions were limited. But all oaths foresworn were no longer binding, he hinted a few days later. His legs felt good again.

His eyes lighted as he considered the prospect of an attack Poli-style — off alone all day, fighting the wind, the heat and the furies by himself, usually unsuccessfully. The Italian rider was clearly tempted. "Attack? I don't know. Maybe. It depends."

Whatever it depended on, it did not happen during the 226.5- kilometer jaunt past enormous crowds from the start in Hendaye to the finish in Bordeaux. "Not today," Poli said later, jauntily.

In the heavy heat and sleep-inducing trip past long stretches of pine forests, the winner was Frédéric Moncassin of the Gan team, a sprint winner nearly three weeks earlier and the wearer of the yellow jersey before the Tour got serious. Erik Zabel of Telekom and Fabio Baldato, an Italian with MG, both were inches behind in the traditional sprint finish in Bordeaux.

While others in the mass rush to the line were swinging and swaying, Moncassin held to a straight and clear line to get his wheel across first after 5 hours 25 minutes 11 seconds of labor, an average speed of 41.7 kilometers an hour. Overall, Riis continued as the leader by 3:59 over Ullrich and by 4:25 over Virenque.

In addition to its wines, Bordeaux, in southwest France, is famous as the site of the jewel victory for sprinters in the Tour de France. Almost invariably on the race's itinerary, the city turns out its citizens in huge numbers, especially when, like this day, the finish was downtown, near the Garonne River and the 18th-century houses that serve as headquarters for wine dealers. In recent years, the finish had been moved to an outlying industrial park with all the charm expected of an industral park.

Moncassin, an amiable fellow, was happy to explain to anybody who would listen how he had accomplished his victory. "My teammates helped a lot," he said. "Earlier in the Tour, I had nobody to lead me out because Gan is not used to working for a sprinter. They haven't had one before me. So I had to do the work for myself. But still, they're not Telekom, Saeco or TVM — teams that know how to set up a sprinter. So I've learned how to look out for myself and it's better that way."

For the next season, although he did not know it then, Moncassin would be getting some help for the leadout: Months later, Gan announced that Eros Poli would be transferring from Saeco to its jersey. Yes, that Eros Poli.

Even though Bordeaux was not Poli's day, he had one more chance: July 21, when the 83rd Tour completed its three-week journey to Paris. Would he launch himself there? "Just wait and see," he replied pleasantly.

That was not the response of the Poli who, off-handedly, like a man telling why he had to scratch an itch, explained a few days before the Pamplona stage why he had to attack soon in the Tour de France. Although he had made a few brief sorties since the Tour began, they did not count, since he joined other riders. Vintage Poli was solo Poli.

"Until now," he said, "it wasn't easy for me to attack. The first days, when it was raining, there was always a headwind. You cannot attack with a wind in your face. Now it's better. I like the sun much more. And Cipollini has gone home, so

I have no team work to do. I'm ready to attack. I'm only waiting for a good moment."

Poli, then 32 and riding for the Saeco team headed by the extroverted sprinter Mario Cipollini, waited every Tour for a good moment. He usually found one. Two years earlier, he attacked on a flat stage to the western outpost of Futuroscope, stayed away alone for hours, and was finally caught almost within sight of his goal.

Occasionally his moment is an especially good one. Days after the Futuroscope fugue, he attacked alone on a stage distinguished by a long, steep and discouraging climb up Mont Ventoux. Knowing that Poli, who stands 6 feet 4 inches and weighs 189 pounds, was far too big to climb, the pack let him build a lead exceeding 20 minutes at the foot of the Ventoux. Astonishingly — he himself was astonished, he admits — Poli made it up the mountain in heavy heat, threw himself over the summit, and used his weight to speed down the descent and finish a winner by 3:39.

In the mountains, Poli was usually the man who led in the stragglers, setting the pace in the long *gruppetto*, as the line of straggling riders is called in Italian, or *autobus*, as it is called in French. He calculated how far behind the winner the trailing group could finish to avoid disqualification and set his speed accordingly and unerringly.

This was his fourth Tour and he had finished two previously. When he spoke a few days from the finish, getting to Paris was not his primary goal. First came the awaited attack, victorious or not.

"I have to try," he said. But what if he ran out of chances? "Impossible," he replied.

Stage 20

TO USE HIS OWN WORD, Chris Boardman had experienced a disappointing Tour de France and now, like so many other riders, he was looking forward to the Olympic Games for solace.

"I don't see any reason why I shouldn't have a good performance at the Olympics," he said. "Whether it will be good enough, I don't know." Never boastful, he spoke more tentatively than usual. Thirty-ninth place overall in the Tour, nearly an hour and a half behind the leader, tends to breed humility.

So did a sixth place in the final long time trial, 63.5 kilometers from Bordeaux to the furnace of the St. Emilion wine district. If grapes need a blazing sun, 1996 should be a great vintage.

Because he was so far down in the standings, Boardman left in the individual race against the clock far before the overall leaders. Although he posted the best time — 1 hour 18 minutes — of the first clutch of 129 starters, he was eclipsed once the main contenders began to finish.

The easy winner was Jan Ullrich, the second-placed rider and the revelation of the 83rd Tour. He was clocked in 1 hour 15 minutes 31 seconds in the bake-off (temperatures high 90s), or an average speed of 50.4 kilometers an hour. Second was Indurain, who finished 56 seconds slower than Ullrich and remained in 11th place overall, where he would be once the Tour concluded its ceremonial 21st and last stage the next day in Paris. Olano was third, 2:06 back.

"Before today, I had never ridden a time trial longer than 50 kilometers," Ullrich said. "All I wanted was to keep my place in the overall standings." He did far better than that, showing remarkable freshness after his first Tour and leaving the widespread impression that, not to turn 23 until December, he was the major rider of the years ahead.

The German had started the race almost unknown — a victory in the 1993 amateur world road-race championship, and a third place in the 1994 world time trial championship his major accomplishments — and had shown that he could climb as well. Unlike most young riders in their first Tour, he was not there for limited experience and a dropout halfway along. That had not been his desire all that season when he nagged his *directeur sportif*, Walter Godefroot, for a Tour berth.

A month before the Tour, he had still not made Telekom's team. Then, in the Tour of Switzerland, where he finished 19th and handled the mountains well, he impressed Godefroot, who bumped Peter Meinert from the roster for Ullrich. "I think I made the right decision," the *directeur sportif* said coyly weeks later.

Showing signs of fatigue and overheating in the second half of the race against the clock, Riis finished a somewhat disappointing fourth, 2:18 down but good enough to retain the yellow jersey. His lead over Ullrich was reduced, however, from 3:59 to 1:41. Barring mutiny on the Champs-Elysées, there it would stay. The only change in the overall standings involved Leblanc of Polti and Fernando Escartin, a Spaniard with Kelme, who switched places as Leblanc moved from eighth to sixth.

Both Ullrich and Indurain were doubtful for the Olympic Games. The German had to choose between the Games and the Tour because his national cycling federation thought he was too young to race both. Indurain had been saying that he would go to Atlanta only if he felt he could win the time trial there.

He reaffirmed that position after the St. Emilion time trial, which was conducted over rippling terrain before huge crowds enjoying an all-afternoon lunch at the edge of the vineyards. "Atlanta is doubtful because my legs do not feel strong over a long distance. Up to 40 or 50 kilometers, I felt good today, but not longer." The Olympic time trial in Atlanta two weeks later would cover 52.2 kilometers.

If he did not go, a favorite in that race would be Boardman, just turned 28. The 52.2-kilometer time trial had a special significance to him — it was exactly the distance he covered in July 1993 when he set the world record for the hour's ride against the clock. That record had since been broken by Indurain and then Rominger.

Boardman planned to skip the long road race July 31 in the first Olympic Games open to professional bicycle riders.

"I'm not confident, no," he said of his chances in the time trial. "You'll have the Indurains, the Romingers and riders of that quality there. But I think I have a damn good chance. To do the time trial fresh, a one-off, one-hour blast is not the same as after 17, 18, 19 days of racing in the Tour."

His third Tour, and the first one he would finish, had been difficult, Boardman admitted. "Sometimes it can be like any other race and sometimes it can be the hardest thing you've ever done," he said.

Describing the stage into Pamplona as "suffering for eight hours," he called it "the most unpleasant experience I've ever had." He finished more than 45 minutes behind, in 116th place, and his main solace was that medical tests halfway through the race showed that he was somehow not getting the full benefits of carbohydrates in his diet.

The Briton needed time to recover, which was another reason he planned to skip not only the pursuit three days after the Tour, but also the road race. As he knew, he had little chance on the road.

On paper, where races are never conducted, the Belgians had one of the strongest five-man entries in the road race, since four of their riders came from the Mapei team and knew how to work together. But Georgia's heat and humidity were likely to unhinge the Belgians, who were far more accustomed to the strong and frigid winds of home.

Similarly, the United States would be represented by four Motorola racers, including Armstrong, Hincapie and Andreu. Italy invariably sent a strong team to the world championships and would do so at the Games, even if the number of riders would be half those at the Worlds, and thus theoretically unable to control the race and set up a finish for the team's sprinter, Cipollini.

Whether the road race, which had only one small elevation, would come down to a mass sprint finish was much debated among Tour riders. Most thought so, but there were some dissenters, notably Sorensen, who was not a strong sprinter, although he could ride all day and night, if need be, at the front on the flat.

Naturally, he foresaw a race for tough riders like himself. Sorensen was especially motivated. While he had not competed in the Olympics before, his father had — in 1964 as a member of the Danish bicycle pursuit team.

Stage 21

VICTORIOUS IN THE TOUR DE FRANCE, Bjarne Riis rode across the last finish line in Paris with his arms upraised in a V and some big questions in his slipstream.

First, how did Riis progress to dominating winner of the three- week Tour after he floundered in two races half that long just a month before?

Second, what happened to Miguel Indurain, who had won the five previous Tours before he slid down to 11th place, 14 minutes 14 seconds behind?

Last in, first out: Indurain appeared to have been the victim of many factors, including age, weather, a weak team and, most startlingly, a lack of peak condition.

"Last year he looked ripped, like lean," said Frankie Andreu. "You looked at him and 'Holy cow, man, he can rip the cranks off the bike.' This year you didn't see that kind of definition. During the race, you could see he was suffering a little bit more, struggling."

After the first 10 days were marked by nearly incessant cold rain, Indurain found too late the heavy heat he needed, and was unable to shed a bit of extra weight he brought to the Tour. While it was no more than a kilogram and a half (about three pounds), which he expected to lose quickly in the usual Tour heat, even that little made a major difference in the mountains to a rider of Indurain's size: 6 feet 2 inches and 176 pounds.

The weight and the bad weather, combined with a team lacking Indurain's usual locomotives to help him over the first climbs in the mountains, reduced his chances of a record sixth victory in the Tour. So did the odds. Four men — Anquetil, Merckx, Hinault and Indurain — had each won the Tour five times, and only Indurain had won consecutively. None of them had won at the age of 32 or older.

Indurain also ran out of his legendary luck. Never during his five victories had he been sick or had a crash or, seemingly, even a flat.

"Of course, he creates his own luck," Lance Armstrong had explained before the start. "Nothing fazes him. He doesn't get into crashes because he's got four or five guys around him all day long. He's always out of trouble."

That did not resemble the Indurain of the 1996 Tour, the one who rarely had any teammates around him, the one who had a flat just as he started to attack, the one who ran out of energy on the first day in the Alps. In all his previous Tours, the worst accident that he had experienced, and the only time he showed anger, was when another rider stepped on his foot as he changed shoes after a stage. This time, his fortunes were so low that, as he waited on the road after another flat, he was run into by a press photographer's motorcycle.

No, the fates had turned the other way for his 32nd birthday.

Then how did Riis emerge at that age to beam as a French military band launched into "There Is a Lovely Country," his national anthem, to salute the winner? Apparently, the Dane was a late bloomer, a rider who avoided the pressures and responsibilities of leadership until 1996. Before that he was a support rider and a lieutenant — always Tonto to some Lone Ranger or other — in France and Italy. Although he had won stages in the Giro d'Italia and the Tour de France, his overall victory in the Tour was his first major one in a 10-year professional career.

Not unkindly, his performance could have been described as a triumph of the ordinary. Riis proved that just showing up really was a major part of life. In its way, his victory was inspirational: There was nobody in a job so humble and unrewarding that he could not look at the Dane, glowing in his yellow jersey, and think "It could happen to me too." Riis had never shown promise of stardom, never been more than a worker bee, a 9 to 5 kind of guy who brought his lunch from home to save a few pennies. Now he stood on a podium overlooking the

Champs-Elysées, regal. He was a people's champion, testimony to the creed of just stick with it, just do your job, something good will happen, maybe.

When he joined Telekom, he announced that his only goal was to win the Tour. He started on that path slowly, and was still unimpressive a month earlier. "In the Dauphiné and the Tour of Switzerland," where he was left far behind in June, "I was sick," Riis explained. "Not until the championship of Denmark did I find my best form."

He won that race, and for the first nine days of the Tour wore the red jersey with white cross of the Danish champion. Then he donned the luminous yellow jersey of the overall leader of the Tour, never to lose it during the rest of the 3,900-kilometer journey.

In the usual sprint finish on a hot, sunny, and festive day on the Champs-Elysées, Fabio Baldato, an Italian with MG, was first across the line among the 129 riders remaining of the 198 who started the Tour. Second was Moncassin, and third was Jeroen Blijlevens. The pack came in bunched despite the equally usual series of breakaways in Paris — including a doomed and short one by Eros Poli that preceded one by Richard Virenque that gave him the points necessary to win the Tour's designation of most aggressive rider.

A crowd estimated at half a million saw Baldato end the 147.5-kilometer roundabout spin from the town of Palaiseau in 3 hours 30 minutes 44 seconds, a speed of 41.9 kilometers an hour. In a change of the traditional itinerary, the riders not only traversed the Champs-Elysées eight times as usual, but also passed the Invalides, the Place de la Bastille and the Place du Châtelet, among other tourist attractions.

Tens of thousands of Danes, all of them exuberant, and some possibly sober, traveled to Paris in buses plastered with Riis banners to help celebrate the first victory by a Dane since the Tour began in 1903.

Riis closed the proceedings by finishing 1:41 ahead of Ullrich, with Virenque third and the first Frenchman since 1989 to stand on the final podium. Another Frenchman, the much and justly maligned Luc Leblanc, finished sixth, giving citizens of the host country a day to crow about. They did, they did.

For his victory, Riis collected 2.2 million French francs (about $400,000) from a total prize pool of more than 12 million francs. Virenque got 150,000 francs for being the best climber and 600,000 for finishing third. Erik Zabel wore the final green jersey of the points champion, worth 150,000 francs. Ullrich received 1.1 million francs for finishing second and 100,000 as the best rider under 25.

Added to the money each received on a daily basis for wearing the various jerseys and winning five stages, it amounted to quite a haul for Telekom. The year before, the German team had been admitted to the Tour at the last moment and had to share a berth with ZG Mobili from Italy. Then, over the winter, Riis was signed on as leader and the blitzkrieg began.

What did it mean for the future? Was the Indurain era over and the Riis era, or the Ullrich era, or the fill-in-the-blank era, just starting? The winner had only this to say: "Next year I would like to beat Miguel Indurain when he is at 100 percent."

7
Atlanta '96

SEAN YATES THOUGHT he would never get another chance at the Olympics. So did Lance Armstrong, Chris Boardman, and George Hincapie — they believed they had raced there with varying success, turned professional, and were ever after ineligible. The Games were for amateurs.

"Were" is the word. In 1996 the distinction between amateurs and professionals was swept aside in bicycle racing and the Games were open to all riders. A few professionals raced on the track in sprints, pursuit, and the points race, but most concentrated on the time trial and the road race. The Tour de France came first, on the calendar and in their affections, but riders were generally eager to make their national teams and compete in Atlanta.

Take, for example, Yates, the strong and durable British racer, who was not overly happy the first time he went to the Olympics. "That was in 1980," he said, "and it wasn't so much fun because it was in Russia. They tended to keep us apart from the people. We were all pretty enclosed in the Olympic Village." Nor did he win any medals: fifth in individual pursuit on the track and sixth in team pursuit.

He turned professional between those Games and the ones in Los Angeles in 1984 and never imagined he would have another chance to be an Olympic athlete. But early in the spring, Yates, who was selected for the British five-man team in the road race, could hardly wait to get to Atlanta before the start of that race on July 31.

"It'll be more fun, everything around the actual race, in America," he believed. "Everyone will be there and the whole world will be watching."

Sharing his enthusiasm was his team leader, Armstrong, who said, "They're in America and they're the Olympics. The combination of the two is big. I think it excites all the professionals." Armstrong finished a disappointing 14th in the road race in the 1992 Games in Barcelona, Spain. "Never did I think I'd get another chance," he said.

Just as excited was Hincapie, Armstrong's teammate with Motorola and with the U.S. team in the Atlanta road race. Hincapie, who raced the team time trial in the '92 Games, lived in Charlotte, North Carolina, so had a special interest in participating. "It's Atlanta, just four hours from my house," he said. "Riding there is a big goal for me. Not just make the team but do something in the Olympics."

Not everybody was that carried away. Boardman put the season in perspective: "The Tour de France obviously comes first," both in priorities and timing. Boardman was not able to defend the pursuit championship he won in Barcelona. "I can't. The pursuit is three days after the Tour de France, on the other side of the Atlantic, six hours' time difference — it's just not possible." Instead, he would ride the time trial, in which he was world champion in 1994. That race, over 52.2 kilometers, was scheduled August 3. "If you come out of the Tour in good shape, there is no better preparation."

Team officials agreed with that and with the value of an Olympic championship. "I've told our riders if they have a chance to go, they must go," said Patrick Lefevere, the Belgian who coaches the powerhouse Mapei team, mainly Belgian and Italian riders. "If you're Olympic champion, you're a champion for four years — that's a lot of publicity." But none of the top contenders in the Tour held back because of the Games.

"Maybe some of the sprinters will drop out in the mountains to save themselves for the Olympics," said Yates, anticipating Cipollini's withdrawal, among others. "But I don't see anybody else, any of the overall leaders doing it. The mountains can only help them in view of the Atlanta road race."

Boardman agreed. "There are unlikely to be any dropouts in the Tour except perhaps sprinters," he felt. "The course in Atlanta is flat, so it may be a race for sprinters."

The race on July 31 was long — 221.5 kilometers — and expected to be hot and humid — Atlanta in summer. "A strong guy will win," perhaps even a sprinter, Yates predicted. One reason is that national teams did not have 10 or a dozen riders, as they did in the world championships, but only five, not nearly enough to dictate tactics and chase down breakaways. "That will make it very open," the Briton added.

"The course is not so hard, discounting weather conditions, so it will be a bit of a free-for-all, I think. The course is undulating so up to the two-thirds distance it'll be pretty wild. Then at the end the strong guys are going to come through."

Armstrong hoped to be one of those strong guys, just as he was when he won the world championship road race in Oslo, Norway, in 1993. But, he said, "It's a one-day race and you can't bet the whole year on a one-day race."

Nevertheless, he admitted that he was upbeat about his prospects and the Olympic Games themselves.

"In Barcelona, in '92, we were stuck out in the countryside," he said. "This should be exciting, being right in Atlanta. That's the good thing about the course, that it's right in town and there should be a lot of people there, a lot of Americans, a lot of support, I hope."

There was a lot of support — about 150,000 spectators — during the road race, as he expected, but nothing else went according to the script. The weather, for example, turned out to be comfortable in the 70s rather than scorching, and the feared humidity dissipated in some early showers.

In the end, the old adage about the riders making the race was proven once again. All the professionals came to race.

"It seems like organizers try to make the courses so hard that the courses tear apart the riders," said Frankie Andreu. "Instead, the riders in this race tore each other apart."

The first 13-kilometer lap through the Buckhead neighborhood north of downtown Atlanta was timed at more than 45 kph, breaking the Olympic record of 43.3 kph set in 1988 in Seoul, South Korea. The race got even quicker in its second half, with one lap topping 49 kph. The final average speed was 45.2 kph, or a rapid 28 mph.

One prediction proved to be true, that the Olympic winner would have ridden the Tour and reached a peak that absentees could not. Thirty-three kilometers from the finish, Pascal Richard, from Switzerland, Rolf Sorensen, from Denmark, and Max Sciandri, from Britain, broke away from a group of 12 leaders and cruised to the finish; Richard and Sorensen had won stages, and Sciandri had been a constant presence in the Tour.

After a series of early and doomed attacks among the 183 starters, the decisive breakaway formed on the 13th of 17 laps, and Armstrong, who had found himself behind in the pack chasing three riders, including Andreu, was mainly responsible. Moving up through the pack, he suddenly found himself at the front, went off in a three-man counterattack and "a few more guys came up to us and that was it."

With 39 kilometers to go, Armstrong attacked alone from the 12-man front group. "When I turned around, I had a good gap," he told John Wilcockson of *VeloNews*, "and I had Frankie back there. I was hoping for either a smaller group to come up or for them to not get organized. But at the same time, I was hoping I would feel a little stronger.

"I definitely didn't feel super. I was strong when I started to go away, but I couldn't roll it like I hoped."

The American was caught by Richard, with Johan Museeuw and Sciandri just behind. At the start of the climb, Sorensen attacked and only Richard and Sciandri could go with him. Their gap was 10 seconds, and then 26 by the end of the lap. This was the winning break.

Only Andreu was able to close on them, at one point getting within 23 seconds before the leaders saw the American uniform, possibly mistook Andreu for Armstrong, and raised their pace. Alone, Andreu fell back to a position between the lead group and the chasers, who were now more than a minute down. On the last lap, Richard and Sciandri each attacked and was caught. Sciandri tried again 700 meters from the finish and was caught.

With 250 meters left, it was Sorensen's turn to attack, but Richard was too alert and too fast. He passed the Dane in the last 25 meters to become Olympic champion, riding the rest of the season in a specially emblazoned and possibly illegal jersey, with the unhappy Sorensen second and Sciandri third. The gallant Andreu, who had ridden solo so long in his vain chase, managed to hold onto fourth place, 1:14 behind Richard, by a second over Richard Virenque. Armstrong was a disappointed 12th.

A few days later, the final time trial in the recent Tour was replayed with only Jan Ullrich, the winner then, missing. So Miguel Indurain moved up from second place in St. Emilion to first place in Atlanta, clocking 1:04.05 over the 52.2 kilometers, and Abraham Olano moved up from third place to second, 12 seconds slower. Boardman was third, 31 seconds down on Indurain.

Hampered by rain that fell while he was on the course, Maurizio Fondriest of Italy was fourth, with Tony Rominger fifth and Armstrong sixth. "My legs weren't there to win a medal," the American admitted.

Indurain benefitted from riding in the final group of 38 starters, when the sun reappeared and the course dried. He did not sound especially elated afterward. "Winning the Olympics is a historic achievement," said the man who almost had to be bullied to show up in Atlanta, "but it does not have the same history that the Tour has, and I would prefer to win the Tour."

Back From Atlanta

THREE WEEKS AFTER the Olympic Games, Lance Armstrong wanted to talk about other things. "It was difficult to not have done the Tour and just to have trained," he said somewhat testily of his preparation for Atlanta. "The best preparation was to have been at the Tour but it's hard to control those things, especially with weather conditions like that.

"Of course I would have liked to have done better," he said of his 12th place in the road race and sixth place in the time trial, "but it's bike racing. Sometimes it works, sometimes it doesn't."

Subject closed. The past interested him much less than the present and especially the future. The last-minute rescue almost certainly wouldn't occur, he realized at the end of August, the cavalry would not be coming over the hill. Weeks past what was once a firm deadline to find a new sponsor, the Motorola team still was looking for a company to enable it to continue in 1997.

Armstrong was willing to wait a bit longer. He remained hopeful, he said over the phone from the Netherlands, where he was riding in the Tour of Holland, eventually finishing second to Rolf Sorensen.

"I don't know why it shouldn't happen," he said, referring to a reprieve. But, he admitted, he had been saying that since May, when Motorola announced it was withdrawing. Since then, Jim Ochowicz, the team's general manager, had spoken to many potential sponsors and come up empty.

"Och has had four or five people who have led him along, led him along, told him they're definitely going to do his bike team, and then the bottom falls out," Armstrong said bitterly. He noted that Ochowicz was then in the United States on a last attempt.

"If he doesn't find something, then it doesn't say a lot for our sport, both nationally and internationally," he continued. "When we can't keep a high-level American team sponsored by a high-level American company on the stage, it's sad. To me it symbolizes a lot, and it's not good.

"I don't believe the decision-makers at big corporations realize what they're getting when they sponsor a cycling team. It's not Yankee Stadium and it's not the Chicago Bulls, but this is not a charity. This is a great avenue to use.

"We're not desperate cyclists going around begging for money — this is something they can use, they can put their name on it and get $8 in publicity back for their $1."

He had done his best in a corporate sense, he said. "I've done work. I want us to find a sponsor. I've done everything I can to help, dealing with smart people I know in places I know, dealing with people who are well connected, with corporations, people who make decisions." Some of this may have helped, but not much.

September is usually the month that riders announce that they are moving to a new team and Armstrong thought that if he had such news to make public, he would do it then. He was not prepared to make that announcement earlier although, he confirmed, he had made a verbal commitment to a new team if Ochowicz could not find the money to continue.

"I've signed nothing," the Texan said. "But I've narrowed my choices down to one if Jim is ultimately out, which I think he is." A week later, Armstrong announced that he would be leading the new Cofidis team, based in France and directed by Cyrille Guimard, who had led three riders to victory in the Tour de France, although none of them in the last decade. The papers were signed a few days later in Paris.

Attempted talks with the Banesto team in Spain had gone nowhere. "They're not interested. They don't even return phone calls." Negotiations with the Festina team, based in France, fell through in July. "They were interested, but they didn't want to give me the time. They wanted a decision in July and I wasn't prepared to make a decision in July."

After he dropped out of the Tour de France because of illness and returned home to Austin, Texas, Armstrong was notified of Festina's lack of further interest by fax. "That says a lot about the organization," he said. "That's OK. They'll realize soon enough."

The experience, like Ochowicz's with potential sponsors, taught him that a deal is not final until the papers are signed. If the former world road-race champion and double stage winner in the Tour de France still needed to impress any future employer, he rode well in the late summer after his impressive spring.

"It's the best season I've ever had," he decided. "I'm ecstatic about my season. My No. 1 goal was to have a fantastic spring, and in the middle of May I was the

No. 1 rider in the world." That ranking followed his victory in the Flèche Wallonne and the Tour DuPont, and his second places in Liège–Bastogne–Liège and Paris–Nice.

Beginning in July, however, he declined. First he had to quit the Tour de France because he became ill and thought that riding in the constant rain would impede his chances in the Olympic Games. Then in Atlanta he rode honorably if not overwhelmingly.

Since the Olympics, he had been 14th in the Clasica San Sebastian, fourth in the Leeds International Classic, and fourth again in the Grand Prix of Switzerland. Overall, he ranked 10th in the world and fifth in the standings of the World Cup.

Although victory in the World Cup had been one of his goals at the start of the season, he dropped out of competition by mid-September, returning home before the season finished in late October.

"It's not realistic to think you can go from March to November," he said. "I just want to spend some time at home."

His off-season activities, he added, would include French lessons. "I'm prepared," he said. "I'll spend the entire winter tutoring. I don't want to go to a foreign team and be a foreigner. If you're the leader, you have to be able to communicate. I've been in this team five years and seen guys come and go who won't learn English. It just doesn't work. A leader whose teammates see him not even making an effort, you shoot yourself right in the foot."

Armstrong was equally unworried about learning another language early in the Tour, when he first discussed the prospects of moving. "I don't have a problem with languages," he said then. "I've never been forced to learn a language, but if I'm forced, give me two months and I'll have it.

"I thought I would ride my entire career for one team, but if you have a sponsor that stops and you can't find a new one, you have to rethink things and realize 'Hey, I'm going to have to leave, hey, I am going to have to go to a foreign team with a program that I've never seen anything of except in the races.'"

The prospect did not scare him, he insisted. "Not really, no." Nor did the change in food and training that faced him. "Food is food, we all eat the same pretty much. It's pasta. The Italians eat it *al dente* and I do too and so does everyone else except in France, where they don't cook it right. Training, I think, is up to the professional to train how he wants."

Armstrong looked off into the distance then and summed up his outlook: "It'll be a neat challenge," he said, "and I think it will probably be a good thing for my career. It wouldn't be a bad thing for me to leave."

8
Gearing Up
for the Future

THAT WAS A SWELL PARTY they gave before the Paris–Tours race: bouncy music, good food, not-so-good wine but plenty of it, friends not seen since the end of the Tour de France two months before. The only problem was the conversation. It was boring.

Nobody in the small world of bicycle racing wanted to talk about anything except Miguel Indurain. Would he or wouldn't he retire?

Don't even try to talk about the ozone layer or the elections in Bosnia or what exactly is the European single currency and how many people will have to lose their jobs to make it successful. Indurain — was he gone or wasn't he? — had become the sole topic of conversation.

"I turned off the saga a couple of weeks ago," said the Australian rider Neil Stephens, as he imitated a man, click!, switching off the television set.

He was one of the few no longer paying attention. The Big Mig question dominated proceedings at the presentation of teams in Issy les Moulineaux, a suburb of Paris, and at their hotels afterward.

There was no point in trying to find the one man who might have answered the question accurately — Indurain. He never rides in Paris–Tours, 244.5 kilometers of flat, windswept course that invariably ends, as it did this time, in a sprint finish. Nothing about this World Cup classic suits his strengths, and so he stays home in Spain, training.

Not this year, though. He was in Spain, yes, but not training. He was down on the Costa del Sol with his wife, Marisa, and their infant son, Miguel Jr., taking the sun, looking in the windows of souvenir shops, watching the Mediterranean tide, such as it is, come in.

The season would continue another month, including the world road race and time trial championships, but Indurain had nothing on his schedule except a series of exhibition races in Spain.

Some people regarded those races as his farewell to the countrymen who have cheered him through five successive victories in the Tour de France. Others thought the races were just a nice gesture and, at $25,000 an appearance, a lucrative one.

After that? He was not saying. Indurain had an option year on his contract with the Banesto team, which paid him about $3.5 million annually, and had told anybody who asked that he did not yet know whether he would continue to race. He would decide in November, he said. And, if the answer was yes, he would also decide then which team he would represent next season.

After a dozen years with the same management under different sponsors' jerseys, he was so hurt and angry that he was willing to listen to other offers. The line formed to the left: ONCE, Banesto's main rival in Spain, started wooing him intensely during the Vuelta a Espana.

The Vuelta was where all the talk about his possible retirement began. It was not a good race for Indurain, who knew it would not be a good race for him.

"My legs felt like blocks of wood," he said when he quit the Vuelta during a hard mountain stage. "It was impossible to breathe."

He had conferred with his Banesto team's doctor a couple of times during the stage before he simply pulled off the road at the team's hotel, 30 kilometers from the finish. Adios Vuelta.

"I had worse days in the last Tour de France," he admitted. "But the law of our sport is very hard, and when you don't have good health, nothing good follows," he said in l'Equipe.

"These things happen in sports," he continued. "Bicycle racing, even when you're a professional, is only a sport. There are more serious things in life."

There went possibly his last attempt to win the only big Tour that had eluded him, the one in his own country. Five times the winner of the Tour de France, and twice the winner of the Giro d'Italia, he has finished no better than a distant second in the Vuelta.

Indurain had not even ridden in it the last few years, preferring to focus instead on the Tour de France and then the world championships. He did not intend to participate this season either, but he was forced to by his team.

That was indignity No. 2, following the major humiliation of his career, 11th place in the Tour and his dreadful 19th place on the stage into Pamplona, when hundreds of thousands of Spaniards turned out to see the local boy make good. When he finished more than eight minutes behind the winner, did his heart break in two or 22?

Next on the schedule were the Olympic Games, which, pleading exhaustion, he wanted to skip. Only an unpublicized appeal by Juan Antonio Samaranch, the

Spaniard who heads the International Olympic Committee, and by King Juan Carlos of Spain persuaded Indurain to go to Atlanta, where he won the time trial.

People wrote then that Big Mig was back, not understanding that the results almost exactly duplicated the finish two weeks earlier in the Tour's last time trial, when Indurain finished second, and Abraham Olano third, to Jan Ullrich. With Ullrich absent in Atlanta, Indurain moved up to first, and his countryman Olano to second.

Then came the forced participation in the Vuelta. "In 12 years as a professional," he said, "it's the first time the team has imposed its wishes on me, the first time the team has not let me decide my own program. I'm very disappointed that they don't trust me. If I say that I'm exhausted, why should they doubt it?"

Indignity No. 3 preceded the start of the Vuelta when it became known that the Banesto team was trying to recruit Olano, who looks like Indurain, often rides like him and, at 26, was six years younger than him.

Even if the Olano deal had not been signed, the implication was obvious: Banesto believed Indurain no longer could win the Tour de France and wanted another leader, in fact if not in name. Big Mig could spend his last season grooming his successor, maybe even help him win the Tour de France.

So Indurain was taking the rest of the year off, skipping the world championships, where he would have defended his title in the time trial and perhaps, after two second places, finally won the road race, his unspoken dream.

Would he or wouldn't he retire? One guess was that he was too proud to quit so near what was for him the bottom. When he was summoned to the victory podium in Pamplona to satisfy his fans, his body was slack but his eyes flared.

The man is powered by pride. It seemed inconceivable that he was willing to leave quietly with so many indignities waiting, just waiting, to be set right.

In the Big Leagues

VINCENT LAVENU was beaming. He leaned against his Petit Casino team car and regarded the world with satisfaction. Fans, riders, officials, journalists, small children on the shoulders of their parents pushed by and Lavenu smiled at one and all. Noblesse oblige.

"We're a first division team now," he said proudly before the start of the Paris–Tours race in the pretty village of St. Arnoult en Yvelines in the Paris outback. "*Fini*, the second division."

An A team, at long last. No more B team competitions: When the major teams are racing the Tour of Flanders, Lavenu will be there as *directeur sportif*, not in his accustomed Grand Prix de Rennes on the same day in a parallel but minor universe. Rennes! When the big boys are up in Liège–Bastogne–Liège, so will he and his riders be, not in the Tour of Picardy. Picardy!

Adieu Morbihan, the Grand Prix Ouest France in Plouay, the Tour de Poitou-Charentes. Plouay! Morbihan! Hello, Amstel Gold Race, Leeds International Classic, Tour of Lombardy.

"Milan–San Remo!" he exclaimed, referring to the prestigious one-day race in Italy that opens the World Cup season in March. "We'll be there now. The first time. Next season, Milan–San Remo." Tomorrow the world.

A big-budget team, at long last. After five years of directing small-talent teams for such pinchpenny sponsors as Vanille et Mure, a maker of children's perfumes, Chazal, a processor of cold cuts, and Petit Casino, a string of supermarket coffee shops, Lavenu had shucked off the bargain basement cocoon.

"Not Petit Casino next season," he said gravely. "Casino." The difference is more than that between the two of spades, little casino, and the 10 of diamonds, big casino — the difference is first division and second.

Casino is the chain of supermarkets themselves, the many aisles full of paper towels, tinned vegetables, and soft drinks, not the corners given over to coffee drinkers. Even at French prices ($1.50 for a thimbleful of expresso standing at the bar, $2.50 seated), the coffee drinkers could not support a team beyond a budget of 10 million francs ($2 million) a year.

"Impossible," Lavenu explained, a derisory sum when he was bidding for stars against Mapei, ONCE, Banesto, and other teams with budgets more than triple his. But now. He winked an eye.

Although he would not confirm it, Casino was believed to have anted up 25 million francs for his team. "Not to say what all the private sponsors contribute — next year we're Casino but also, still, C'est Votre Equipe. That's very important to note" — he would retain his network of small contributors, his fan support.

"Measured one way, in victories, this has not been a memorable season for us," Lavenu admitted. His voice dropped to the most confidential: "Three victories this year." He brightened, as he always does: "Still, that's three better than none."

Measured another way, though, in what the French call places of honor — which can include second, third, close calls, moral victories, psychologically uplifting performances — this had been a vintage year for Petit Casino. "Many, many places of honor," he reported. "Too numerous to detail."

As a rider himself a decade ago, Lavenu was celebrated for his enthusiasm more than his talent, for his ability to see promise and a fresh beginning where others saw nothing.

"The Tour de France this year, when we did not get the invitation, that turned out to be a good thing for us," he said. "Naturally, the sponsor was disappointed — a French team not in the Tour de France, naturally disappointment."

But Lavenu said what they had to do was build a team that would be invited, no question, next season. "What we need are a big budget, big stars, a big team." The sponsor appreciated his reasoning.

Lavenu found himself that big star, signing Pascal Richard, the 32-year-old Swiss rider who in 1996 won the Liège–Bastogne–Liège classic, a stage in the Tour de France, and then the road race in the Olympic Games at Atlanta. "An exemplary rider," Lavenu said, "a winner, very *mediatique*, a great champion, speaks French from birth.

"Not only Richard, also Saligari, also Jaermann, the best." Marco Saligari, 31, an Italian, and Rolf Jaermann, 30, a Swiss, both strong support riders, would transfer from the MG team in Italy with Richard, bringing with them the points necessary to install a team in the first division.

Richard was attracted to Casino not so much by the money it offered (amount not made public) — "The bidding went up and up, everybody wanted him, but his manager said after a certain level money isn't everything" — but by the chance, Lavenu said, to lead his own team, especially one with spirit. And one, Lavenu did not say, with nowhere to go but up.

"Attention," the coach warned, "we weren't in only small races this year. San Sébastian, we were there. Grand Prix of Zurich, that one too." He did not mention that those World Cup races were open to Petit Casino only because some of the first-division teams declined the honor, and therefore a second-division team like his helped fill out the field at the last moment.

Next season the invitations to Casino would come early. Lavenu smiled, thinking of the next season. Liège–Bastogne–Liège! The Tour of Flanders! Milan–San Remo!

Another Rebirth

BOBBY JULICH, a young and promising American bicycle rider who struggled for the two seasons he had raced in Europe, finally had what he called a rebirth. Again.

"It was another rebirth, no question of that, and I started questioning, 'Why do these things happen to me?'" he said. "The highest of highs, the lowest of lows. You start to question your ability, you start to question your faith."

Not any longer, Julich continued. "My life has changed 110 percent since the Vuelta," the Tour of Spain, in which he finished ninth, rode in the King of the Mountains jersey for 12 days, and gained, he felt, the respect he sought for two empty seasons.

He also gained an employer for the next year once his Motorola team disbanded at the end of the 1996 season. Until he showed in the Vuelta that he could climb with some of the best and finish a demanding three-week race, the 24-year-old native of Glenwood Springs, Colorado, looked as if he might be through in Europe.

"Now I've got offers from five to nine teams," he reported. He eventually chose the new Cofidis team in France. "I'm in no rush, but this sport is unfortunately a What-have-you-done-for-me-lately one, so you have to take advantage of your notoriety.

"I'm not looking to be my own man yet," he continued. "Just because I got ninth in the Vuelta, nobody's going to form a team around me, make me the main guy. But, yeah, I think I do deserve a certain amount of respect now, and it's time to move to the next level. I'm ready to take the next step."

He was standing then in a field in the town of St. Arnoult en Yvelines, signing autographs and chatting with Theo de Rooy, the *directeur sportif* of the Rabobank team. Talking intently, they both looked satisfied.

"If I hadn't had a good Vuelta," Julich said with a smile, "I'd probably be in college right now.

"It was a rite of passage. All the work, all the sacrifices, all the dedication — they do pay off in the end.

"I realized that I never gave 100 percent before. In the past it was 95 percent or 90 percent — 5 percent or 10 percent or whatever percent, that's what makes the difference. Not the big things but the tiny ones. I'm really looking forward to the rest of the season," he said. "There are three weeks and a lot of races left. A lot of people are calling it a season, but I've got great morale and good form and I've got to use them. They don't come very often."

That lesson went back more than the two years in Europe. He started learning it in 1993, which he spent riding in the United States as an independent professional without a team, a sponsor, or a support staff. He was alone in a team sport. The results — none, including the loss of $25,000 of his savings to fund his efforts — were predictable.

A rider who finished fifth in the Tour DuPont in 1991, when he was 19 years old and a member of the U.S. national amateur team, and then 10th in that race the next year, he had offers to join European teams when he turned professional in 1993. But, wary of racing in Europe at that young an age, he accepted instead a job with a new American team to be sponsored by Rossin, an Italian bicycle company.

The team collapsed in January, before the season started, but too late for Julich to find another berth. Going alone from race to race, he lasted till late summer. "And I finally cracked mentally and financially," he said later. He retreated to his home in Santa Rosa, California, fell into what he described as a major depression, and spent the rest of the year watching television.

In 1994 he tried again. A contract with the Chevrolet–L.A. Sheriff team gave him the opportunity to show bigger teams that, at 22, he could still ride strongly and win races. Motorola signed him for the next two years to support Lance Armstrong, his former teammate with the U.S. amateurs.

"Last year, when I came over I was very intimidated," he said. "The European lifestyle — I was very, very nervous about coming over here. To be honest, I was just underprepared.

"The whole year, I kept thinking I would be able to just jump right in at that level, and it wasn't true. I was suffering all year."

The result was a series of washouts, including the Tour of Switzerland, where Julich said he was "murdered, I barely made it through," and the world championships in Colombia, where "something hit me, I was devastated, I couldn't move practically, I got dropped on the first lap and dropped out on the second."

In 1996 he tried again. "I went to the DuPont with great morale and one objective only: to do the work for Lance. I knew it would be difficult, I knew from Day One I would be the main guy to do the work, and I accepted that: it was what I wanted to do. I don't regret it. I learned from it.

"I had never done that work before, I was on the front more than I had been in my whole career combined," riding 10 days solely for his team leader, setting a pace so fast that attacks by rivals were discouraged.

"But that left me totally wasted. I was supposed to have a break then but it was an Olympic year," and he had to ride in the trials to select a U.S. five-man squad. "Two days after the DuPont I went out and was stuck to the road. Mentally I was fresh, but the first race in Seattle it felt like I had mountain bike tires on. I was tired, I needed to cool my jets for a while."

About a week after that, he went to another Olympic trial race, in Pittsburgh, and had what he refers to as "this episode." His heart started racing at 220 beats a minute. "It was the third lap," he remembered, "coming down from the big climb, and I closed my eyes and thought, Please, God, don't let this happen now."

He got off his bicycle and sprawled on the side of the road. "I was lying there on my back for about three hours with my heart going through the roof."

Julich was taken to a hospital, but he knew what the trouble was. "I told the doctors it was diagnosed as PAT, an abbreviation for something long that's just a rapid heartbeat. I had it happen on and off for years. In high school, I had it happen most of the time I wasn't doing anything — lying on my bed or taking a test in school. It's not fatal. I had the smarts to check that out when I was young. But when your heart starts beating 220, 230, just spastically, you feel totally drained.

"It had never got in the way of my cycling before. But it was happening more frequently. It used to be one or two times a year, but in the six months prior to this episode, it had happened five or six times, way over the quota. At the back of my mind, I had thought, 'This can happen anytime. What if this happened half a mile away from the world championship?'"

The Highest of Highs

DEADPAN, WITH NO SIGN of embarrassment or presumption, Bobby Julich repeated his goals, his highly ambitious goals, in the Vuelta a España. For a bicycle racer who had little to show during his first two years in Europe, he was preparing an exploit.

"Hennie Kuiper came into my room before the Vuelta," he said, referring to the Motorola team's *directeur sportif*, a man who had won the Olympic and world championship himself, not to mention the esteemed Paris–Roubaix race, and twice finished second in the Tour de France. "He said, 'I want to know what you want to do in this race.'

"I wanted to tell him, 'Hennie, I'm going to get top 10 and I'm going to take this race by storm, do what I need to do, get a contract for next year and show everyone for the first time, if they question my ability, that I do deserve a spot in the pro *peloton*.' But of course I couldn't say that to Hennie Kuiper. So I said, uh, I want to do well, let's see how it goes and, uh, maybe go for a stage here or there."

Sitting in his hotel before Paris–Tours, Julich finally allowed himself a satisfied smile. Modest and courteous, he could tell his story without worrying that he sounded cocky, because the Vuelta had ended a week before and this was what he did: finish ninth, wear the best climber's jersey for a dozen days, take the race by storm, get a contract for the next year, and win universal respect.

More, he came out of the Vuelta with such good form and high morale that he was still riding like a rocket. Julich finished 11th a week later in the world road-race championship in Lugano, Switzerland, the one-day summit of the professionals' year. "I wanted top 10," he said later, "but I'll take 11th. I'm happy. It's a lot different than I'm used to."

The easy winner, in a two-man sprint, was Johan Museeuw, who celebrated his 31st birthday by beating Mauro Gianetti for the right to wear the rainbow-striped jersey for a year. Museeuw, the leader of the Mapei team and of the World Cup competition for the second successive year, completed the 252-kilometer course, which included two steep but short hills, in 6 hours 23 minutes 49 seconds.

Gianetti, who was born in Lugano and had the vast Italian-speaking crowd with him, finished a second behind. Third place went to Michele Bartoli, of Italy, who was just ahead of Axel Merckx, both of them 29 seconds slower than Museeuw.

Julich was the only Amercan left in the main chasing group, finishing 1:26 behind with such stars as Bjarne Riis, Laurent Jalabert, Tony Rominger, and Gianni Bugno. That was not at all the sort of company he usually kept.

"I was at the front when the good break went," he said, "and I made a little mistake letting that break go. You get so many guys coming by and then they're 15 meters up the road. Before I could react, they were gone. All I could do was hope it would come back."

That it did not was the fault of the French team, notably Jalabert, Richard Virenque, and Luc Leblanc, who did not want to ride for each other and preferred — so French — to lose rather than help a rival win. "It was disappointing," Julich said. "The French wouldn't do anything to get a chase going, but sat there, watching each other.

"It's disappointing," he repeated, "but 11th, I'll take it."

Julich had come a long way in a month, and not just literally, Spain to Switzerland. When he began the three-week Vuelta in September, he was one of the more obscure Motorola riders, far down in the computerized standings, which are based on results. Of those, he had few.

His opportunity came during the second stage in Spain. The night before, he related, Kuiper said to the team that the Motorola car was 17th in the line of march, based on team standings. "'Come on guys,' Hennie said, 'this is ridiculous, 17th.' And I thought, 'OK, I can do something.'"

"I felt real good," he continued breathlessly, "and I saw a little climb about 5 kilometers before the first bonus sprint, and I went for it, thinking I may be able to get that one before they catch me and then it turned into, Oh, wow, I can get the second one, and I got the second one, and I was committed.

"Then I just dropped anchor because there was no way I could try to go to the finish. But I thought I got the team car moved up, except in the finish somebody sat up and I lost six seconds — I won six from the bonuses and then had them taken back, so that didn't work out in terms of moving up the car, but it did turn out to be the beginning of a big thing for me."

Those two small climbs had put him in the white King of the Mountains jersey in the Vuelta, which, like the Tour de France, spends at least its first week on the flat. Over fourth- and third-category climbs, no more than short hills, Julich stayed in the jersey until the big mountains began more than halfway through the race.

He survived such challenges as having to contest every hill and being deliberately crashed into a crowd of spectators, where he landed head first and was saved from grievous harm because he was wearing a helmet. "Konichev crashed me — I was coming around him and he just slammed me into the crowd, pretty blatantly too," he explained, referring to Dimitri Konichev, a Russian with Aki who was second in the climbing competition. "I gained a lot of respect from riders by getting up and not coming to blows with the guy but re-establishing myself by winning the next sprint." By the end of the race in Madrid, he was an easy top 10.

The Vuelta, he felt, was the first race of his professional career where he arrived in peak form and morale, stayed focused, worked mainly for himself, and had a bit of luck besides.

Everything started coming together, Julich said, that day during the Olympic trials in June in Charlotte, North Carolina, when, feeling tired a week after he collapsed with the runaway heartbeat that had troubled him half his life, he went to have his blood tested.

"The doctor was involved with cycling and he mentioned that he heard I had this condition, and he asked did I want to have it treated because, he said, there's this new procedure developed right here. I said, 'Tell me more.'"

After an examination at a hospital in Charlotte, he was told that he had AV, for arterial veinal, Modal Reentry, which the rider defined: "The electromagnetic pulse that makes your heart beat is a line of energy, and I had an auxiliary pathway that allowed it to go back up and around, instead of just down, in a vicious circle. Instead of down and back up the normal circuit, it gets caught right there and literally starts short circuiting."

Julich explained that the condition was not congenital but had been caused, he thought, when he was 12 and was hit above the heart by a hard pass with a football. His options, the doctors in Charlotte said, were medication, a dubious choice for an athlete in a sport with drug controls, simply to ignore it as he had been doing, or a new surgical technique.

Two days later, at 7:30 in the morning, Julich was checking in at Duke University Hospital in Durham, North Carolina. By noon he was out.

Five catheters had been inserted in a vein through a cut on his right thigh that Julich said was no bigger than a pin. Moving the catheters to his heart, the doctors "were looking for the renegade cell, which they had to zap. They go in with a radio wave and try to splice this line of energy so it can't conduct any more.

"I came out of the anesthesia at one point and I looked up and saw all these people with masks on and there was the television monitor and I asked a nurse, 'Is that my heart?' and she said, 'Yeah.' There were five catheters surrounding the area and looking as if they were moving in for the strike. What they were doing was graphing it down until they found the renegade cell, which they had to zap.

"It's very tricky because it's such a small thing. And the burn — any time you burn something in the heart, there are risks involved. The 99.8 percent success rate is great, but what if you're that 0.2 percent where something goes wrong?

"They made three burns, got it on the third burn, let you rest a while, come back at it again and try to stimulate it by injecting an electromagnetic beat — or injecting adrenalin, because adrenalin can also cause it — and it didn't kick up, so they knew they'd got it.

"It was so simple. And just two, three days off the bike. I was a little sore where they put the catheters in, and I was limping around, but it was amazing. I felt like I never have to worry about this again."

He went home then to California and resumed training. "I had fantastic motivation," he said. "All I concentrated on was the Tour of Spain. I wrote it down in August: I can be top 10 in the Vuelta."

And then he was. "Twelve days in the King of the Mountains jersey," he remembered, "12 jerseys, a long-sleeve jersey, a skinsuit — I never won those things before.

"But being on the podium for 12 days, you get 12 sets of flowers and I'd always find a nice old lady at the side of the road to give the flowers to. Trying to brighten up her day a little bit."

Goodbye to All That

GEORGE NOYES, the Motorola team's chief mechanic, called it "The end of an era or something like that," trying to sound chipper. "Life goes on," added Geoff Brown, one of his assistants. "One door closes, another opens, hopefully," said Paul Sherwen, the team's publicity director.

Noyes and Brown had been selling bicycles off the back of the Motorola truck at the last few races of the season. They would willingly have sold the truck too, but it had already been bought by the new Cofidis team.

Everything must go since the team must. For $500, about $1,000 less than it was worth, a friend of the team — and who wasn't? — could have Sean Yates's training bike. It was pretty used but so, in truth, was Yates, who, at 36, was planning to retire to his home in Britain even if the team had been able to find a new sponsor.

Jesus Montoya, 33, was also retiring, to Spain. Lance Armstrong, Frankie Andreu, Bobby Julich, Bruno Thibout, and Kevin Livingston had signed with Cofidis in France; Laurent Madouas with Lotto in Belgium; Max Sciandri, Andrea Peron and Flavio Vanzella with La Française des Jeux, another new French team.

Axel Merckx had said yes to Polti in Italy. George Hincapie was going with U.S. Postal Service, Gord Fraser with Mutuelle de Seine et Marne in France. Somebody thought Max Van Heeswijk would join Rabobank in the Netherlands. Kaspars Ozers seemed to be unaccounted for.

The riders, a generally young and talented bunch, would make out fine. What of all the others — the team officials, masseurs, mechanics, the doctor? So many uncelebrated people, the ones who made it work. In its six years of Motorola sponsorship, the team was highly regarded for its precise organization, its ability to get different groups of riders to their scattered races in comfort, without the helter-skelter atmosphere many other teams endure.

What happened now to the ones who massaged the riders, picked them up at the airport, adjusted the saddle height of their bicycles, inspected their tires, packed and held out lunch bags in the feed zone of so many famous and obscure races, got their luggage to their hotel rooms, found them a glass of milk at 3 A.M., did their laundry, and monitored their training?

Noyes: "I'm taking next year off, recovering, hoping Mr. Ochowicz finds another sponsor for 1998." Late in August, Jim Ochowicz, the team's general manager, gave up his search for a sponsor for 1997 and immediately began looking for one for the year after that. "If he finds a sponsor, we'll start again next August or September, I hope. That's hopefully, that's ideally. It remains to be seen if I can handle standing still for a whole year."

Brown: "I've signed with U.S. Postal Service, so I'll be on the circuit again next year. They're based near Geneva but on the French side of the border, so I'll be moving down there from Belgium. The reality is that everybody needs a job."

Sherwen: "I've had a foot in both camps for the last few years, and now I'll be dedicating a lot more time to my television career: Channel Four in the U.K., ESPN and ABC in America, SABC in South Africa, SBS in Australia. I do a monthly program worldwide called "Velo Magazine," which is a half-hour program. So I've got a lot of work on my plate. I'm also thinking about something I've been dabbling at for a long time, which is a safari company." Sherwen, a former strong professional racer, and once the British champion, grew up in Kenya and Uganda. "I have my own safari vehicle, I've taken people on safari, I've worked in the safari business in Kenya. I'm actually looking to put a brochure together, I'm thinking about it that seriously."

Noel Dejonckheere, European operations manager: "First we have to clean everything up. And then after that I'm going to spend some time with my family, take a holiday, do a bike trip for a week and then do a walking trip with friends around Mont Blanc, four or five days, going from hut to hut. If Jim finds something for '98, we have to start working again."

Eddy DeGroote, part-time *soigneur*, or masseur and jack of all trades, full-time English and Dutch teacher in Belgium: "I have a few contacts, maybe it will be a French team. I've worked with Belgian teams, Dutch teams, an American team, and maybe now it will be a French team."

John Hendershot, head *soigneur*: "Yes indeed, I am retiring and very happily. My wife and I are going to start a boarding kennel for dogs, probably in Colorado but maybe Texas. My wife is an animal trainer by profession and worked in several zoos, including the Bronx Zoo. I'm counting on her to handle the mind work and I'm going to do the shoveling. I resigned in the middle of the year. I'm burned out. This is my 13th year doing it full-time, and my seventh year in Europe with the team. I'd rather leave with people wishing I would stay than stay with people wishing I would go."

Ochowicz: "We're still capable of doing this business, and I'm hoping we find a sponsor. I'll be going back home to Wisconsin to work from there. We have to downsize the corporation to squeeze out six or seven months without income while we try to find that sponsor for 1998."

Massimo Testa, the team doctor: "The last 11 years I took a lot of time from my practice, a family doctor and sports doctor, so maybe it's time to stay a little longer at home in Como. I have no motivation to work for another team full-time. My wife is American, so I would like to start something in the United States as a coach to individual athletes. But I'm always available to work with anybody from this team."

Testa was a youngster working at the University of Pavia in 1985 when the 7-Eleven team, newly turned professional, arrived in his native Italy from the United States to race in the Giro d'Italia. The team's Italian sponsor, Hoonved, a maker of vacuum cleaners, thought a doctor ought to look after the riders in that three-week race.

"They called a doctor who was 50 years old and had worked 20 Giros, but he didn't want to work for the team. He said it was not good for his reputation — he was always working for big teams, not little ones from America that nobody had heard of, and he sent me there instead. It was the first American team in Europe. We won two stages in that Giro, and I've been with them ever since — 11 years.

"It's sad, you know, like a school vacation, everybody going in a different direction. We were a good team, a little different. It was a big challenge to work with people from so many different countries. So I'm happy. I was lucky to have this job. But you know the good times are not coming back."

Testa shook his head, tried a feeble smile. Yes, you knew that about the good times.

9
Off Course

THE PHONE CALL came one morning early in October. "Lance Armstrong will be making an announcement in a conference call later in the day and he'd like you to be part of it," the man from Motorola said. He gave the hour, the phone number, the access code, and would say no more.

In the sport of bicycle racing, a conference call was unprecedented: Good news came through the rumor mill, bad news was covered up. Teams scheduled presentations and sometimes news conferences, but nobody ever had anything with enough priority to warrant a conference call. For a sport that clipped along at 40 kilometers an hour, the day-by-day pace was leisurely. So this had to be big news, bad news, really bad news.

It was. Armstrong revealed from his home in Austin, Texas, that he had testicular cancer, that it had spread to his abdomen and lungs, and that he had started at least 12 weeks of chemotherapy the day before.

"I intend to beat this disease," said the rider, who had celebrated his 25th birthday a few weeks before. "It's impossible to say when I'll be back racing, but I hold out hope to participate at the professional level in the 1997 season.

"I will win," he said. "I intend to ride again as a professional cyclist."

He noted that the survival rate from testicular cancer is 97 percent, but that, "if it spreads, which it has, that number comes down." He said his doctor put his chances of recovery between 65 and 85 percent and described the cancer as "advanced."

"I want to finish by saying that I intend to be an avid spokesperson for testicular cancer once I have beaten this disease. Had I been more aware of the symptoms, I believe I would have seen a doctor before my condition had advanced to this stage. I want this to be a positive experience and I want to take this opportunity to help others who might someday suffer from the same circumstances I face today."

When he finished reading his prepared statement, it was translated into French — the language of bicycle racing and of his new Cofidis team — and then Armstrong took questions, first from the local press who were present at what sounded like a hall in Texas, and then from the international press on the phone.

"I had four hours of chemotherapy yesterday," Armstrong said in answer to a question, "and if I didn't know the diagnosis, I'd feel normal."

Discussing his illness, he said, "It happened very fast." A week before he felt severe pain in a testicle, coughed up blood and went to see a doctor at St. David's Hospital in Austin. After an ultrasound examination, he was told of the cancer and the need to remove the malignant testicle, which was done the next day.

At first he was incredulous. "I'm 25 years old, I'm one of the best in my sport — why would I have cancer? I had lots of tests all through my career, physical tests, blood tests, and they never picked this up.

"This is something I got stuck with and now have to work through," he continued. "I've said all along that I won't live as long as most people, this sport is too hard, the way we push our bodies, extremely over the edge. The Tour de France is not a human event. But it doesn't answer 25.

"I'm entering this battle in the best shape of my life. I'm going to be back on my bike soon, maybe not six hours a day, maybe not as hard as before." He said later that his doctor had approved bicycle riding for up to 50 miles a day as early as the next week.

"I just want to be on my bike, outside, with my friends," Armstrong said. Throughout the hourlong conference call, he sounded buoyant and determined — two qualities, in addition to his talent, that had helped carry him to the top of the sport.

He ranked ninth among the world's approximately 900 professional racers. His biggest victories had been the world road-race championship in 1993, the last two Tours DuPont in the United States, a couple of European classic races, and two stages in the Tour de France. The last of these was in the 1995 Tour, when he crossed the finish line into Limoges, France, with his arms upraised and his fingers pointing to the sky in memory of his teammate, Fabio Casartelli, who had been killed in a crash in the mountains days before.

Answering another question, Armstrong discounted chances that his cancer had affected his performance in the 1996 Tour and caused him to drop out. He noted that he rode well enough in the Olympic Games and then in Europe in August and September. After his fourth places in the World Cup classics at Leeds and Zurich and his second place in the Tour of Holland, he completed his fall with a second place in the Grand Prix Eddy Merckx, a time trial, and two more top five places in time trials. "A month ago, a month ago, I was in Europe competing at the highest level," he pointed out.

"When I came home, I felt a little off, jet lagged, I didn't know what it was. The testicle got a little bigger and then got sore. It was never sore before, so I decided to go in and have it checked.

"Anytime I get a little pain, I blow it off. That's the way I function, that's the way my head is. I wait for it to go away. I didn't know testicles could be a problem. No awareness. That's why I'm going to win this battle, so everybody's going to know."

He was asked then about his contract with Cofidis, reportly worth $1.25 million a year, part of which Armstrong was quietly refunding to the sponsor to help it hire Frankie Andreu, his American friend and teammate with Motorola, whose price tag had risen since his stunning fourth place in the Olympics.

Armstrong said that he did not think he would lose his salary, "but that's something to be worked out in the coming months. I've got bigger things to worry about," he said. "This thing ain't going to stop me. I'm thinking my chances are good. I may have a bald head, but I'll be out there soon on my bike. I'll be out there next week, you'll see."

When he finished, one memory: A reporter interviewing Armstrong in Italy months after he won the world championship heard him say that his victory belonged to all Americans. "I think I'm a little more patriotic than your average American," he explained. "I didn't win the Worlds only for me but for my country too. I feel very American, especially over here, so far from America. I enjoy being American, I take pride in it, being Texan too."

The reporter, an American himself, joked and asked, if the rainbow jersey belonged to him too, when could he wear it?

Shortly after the interview ended, Armstrong excused himself and left the room. He returned a few minutes later and said, "I got something for you, man." It was one of his world champion's jerseys, which he autographed and presented to the reporter. "Really it's for all of us," Armstrong said.

Happy to Be Alive

AS MORNINGS GO, this one in November seemed ordinary: Fog masked the hills west of Austin, Texas, a light wind fluttered flags, the temperature promised another shirtsleeves day. About 7:30 o'clock, rain began falling for half an hour and everybody said that was a good thing because lately there had been a bit of a drought in central Texas.

A commonplace morning for most people, in other words, but another wonderful, joyful morning for Lance Armstrong. He woke at 7 at his home on Lake Austin, went to the kitchen to prepare a pink grapefruit for his breakfast, looked at the morning newspaper and then began celebrating another day of simply being alive.

"Every day I wake up, I feel great," he said later. "I say 'This is great' because six months from now, a year from now, five years from now, I may not be able to say that."

Armstrong had been told seven weeks before that he had testes cancer and that it had spread to his abdomen and lungs. A few weeks later, after the testicular malignancy was removed, he learned that the cancer had gone to his brain, requiring surgery to remove two lessions.

"You can see where they did it," he said. Lifting his blue Dallas Cowboys cap, he leaned forward to show the two stitched semicircles on the top left and the back of his head. Somewhat proudly, he also showed two tiny bumps on either side of his forehead, where screws held his head steady during the five-hour operation.

"I'm feeling fine," he said, "a little bit of fatigue, which means I have to take a nap every day, about two hours. This week I feel like I felt two months ago. I really do. That's no lie.

"I do feel good. I'm not as fit as I used to be, but then again, for two months I haven't done anything on the bike. I'm out of shape, I'm undergoing chemotherapy and I do have cancer, pulmonary lesions that are detrimental. But the lesions on the lungs are going away pretty rapidly.

"I'm really upbeat. I'm positive. I may be a little scared, I may be very scared, but I feel very positive about how things are going."

A few days later Armstrong would leave for a week at the Indiana University Medical Center in Indianapolis to receive four hours of chemotherapy daily for a week. The treatment would be administered through a catheter that was surgically implanted in his left chest and that he wore full-time at home during the two weeks between each of four scheduled weeks of chemotherapy. Taped over his heart, the outside of the device resembles, ironically, the tube that bicycle riders use to pump air into flat tires.

He had no interest in irony, though. He was concentrating on one thing only and that was survival. For him, another morning alive is a triumph.

"It used to be when I woke up every morning, I knew I was going to wake up," he said. "It was so normal I took it for granted, and now I never know. We're not promised anything. We're not promised tomorrow.

"We all expect to have long and fulfilling lives, but I suggest people not take that for granted. We don't always attack life, don't do things to the fullest, and I suggest that people take advantage of life."

He was sitting in the living room of his large, new Mediterranean-style villa, which he helped design and shared with his girlfriend, Lisa Shiels, then a major in chemical engineering at nearby University of Texas.

Circled by palm trees and clumps of flowers, the two-story house is airy and bright with high ceilings, vivid abstract paintings and stylish furniture that he chose with his decorator. This is the house he had dreamed about for years, perhaps as long ago as when he was a teenager living in Plano, outside Dallas, and growing up, as he describes it, "OK, middle class," raised by his mother, a single parent after his father left when Armstrong was an infant.

"This house, it represented a lot," he said in his living room. He had started talking outside, sitting near his swimming pool and hot tub, with a view across Lake Austin. It is also called the Colorado River, he explained, is 20 miles long from a spillway at one end to a dam at the other, and offers fine bass fishing. The view was splendid but the wind that moved the American and Texan flags on his shorefront was too cold for him, and he had to go inside.

Late that June, a couple of months after he moved in, he said, "I'm happier here than I expected to be, and I expected to be very happy." Now that he had cancer, his feelings were more mixed.

"The home, I put a lot into it both in time and money, and I really feel an attachment to this house because this was dirt before, this was level ground and we built it up, furnished it, did everything exactly the way I wanted it.

"When I started it, I must have been 22, and it showed that a 22-year-old can work hard, have success, financially do well, and take on a big project like this and succeed. I've enjoyed it, I enjoy it still. But if it's gone, it's gone.

"Now it means a lot less than it did before. Houses, cars, motorcycles, toys, money, fame — it takes on a whole new meaning when you have something like this," he continued, referring to his cancer. "You realize, 'I never lived for that stuff.' No. I enjoyed it but I think something like this makes you not only look at your life, but makes you simplify your life.

"The home means more than the other things. Before I would have been devastated if I had to sell it or move out to a little old home built in the '30s, much smaller, not on the lake, not in this price range. That's fine. I could do it. That's fine, I'm alive. That's what it's all about."

The tan that he wears during the racing season had disappeared and he seemed pale, understandably less bouyant than usual. He was holding his weight steady at 170 pounds, he said, although he admitted that some of his muscle had turned to fat despite daily bicycle rides of up to an hour-and-a-half.

The weekend before, he even competed, with Eddy Merckx as his partner, in a local race, the 26-mile Tour of Gruene, Texas. "It was a race," he said, "but we didn't race. I can't race right now. I don't know if I can ever race again.

"I wanted to do the race to prove that I was still alive, that I was well, that therapy was ahead of schedule, as well as to prove to cancer patients that cancer doesn't always have to be a killer, therapy doesn't always have to be such a handicap."

Those who knew him best agreed that physically and mentally he was doing well. "He's met every benchmark of progress and there's nothing to keep us from thinking he won't be cured," said Dr. Craig R. Nichols on the phone from Indianapolis. He and Dr. Lawrence Einhorn were treating Armstrong at the Indiana University center.

"Lance's doing great," said Bill Stapleton, his agent in Austin. He had established a mailing address at his law firm, Brown McCarroll & Oaks Hartline, 111 Congress Avenue, Suite 1400, Austin, Texas 78701, for the thousands of get-well wishes that arrive weekly. ("It's indescribable what that means to me," Armstrong said. "I read every last one of them. Those people keeping you in their hopes, their prayers, that positive energy, that makes a difference.")

"He's so upbeat, so confident," said Kevin Livingston, 23, a teammate of Armstrong's in 1996 with the Motorola team, who had moved to Austin to train with him. With the end of Motorola's sponsorship, Livingston followed Armstrong to Cofidis.

"He's doing magnificently," said Linda Walling, Armstrong's mother, on the phone from Richardson, Texas. "It's only a bump in the road. We're going to beat it. I tell him, 'Negatives don't do anything for you but bring you down,' and he knows that. 'Make this the first day of the rest of your life,' I say to him, and that's what he's doing."

Yes, Armstrong agreed, that's what he's doing.

"This is the biggest challenge of my life," he said. "Everything I've ever done has always been up to me. If I want to win a bike race, it's my responsibility to train hard, to eat right, to race smart — all things I could control.

"But now, I'd like to think I can control things, but I don't know, I can only approach them in a way that I feel is appropriate — to fight with my mind and my body and just hope that things work out. I won't make you any guarantees in this fight.

"From the first moment I learned this, I thought, 'Oh my God, I'm going to die.' I went from being at the top of my game, fourth in World Cup races in Leeds and Zurich, to being told I had cancer. Eventually you get over that.

"I said, 'Forget the numbers, forget the chances the doctors give you, forget it. We're going to work hard and we're going to win this. I'm not going to die, I'm going to live.' I chose to live, to fight to live.

"But if you're the biggest, toughest guy out there and saying 'I'm going to live,' there are cases where you do die. Because cancer does not recognize that. It does not play fair. It's aggressive, it's smart, it's tough, it's relentless, it adapts, it becomes resistant to therapies. If it wants to win, it can win."

For now, he continued, he was giving little thought to his career as a bicycle racer, ranked ninth in the world. He had come a long way from the 19-year-old rider on the U.S. national amateur team who fended off questions about whether he was the next Greg LeMond by saying, "No, I'm the first Lance, the first Armstrong." His goals were astronomic: "I know I want to do the Tour de France," he said then, years before his first of four appearances in the world's greatest bicycle race.

"I know I want to win the Tour de France," he continued in that distant past. "I think I can some day get to that level but that's a long way off, a lot of hard work. The desire is there, the ambition is there, the goal is there.

"Win the Tour de France and you're a star. I'd like to be a star," he said, half jokingly. "I'm sure I'd get sick of all the pressure and all the appearances, but I'd like to try it for a while."

Now he had tried it for a while and, even though he had never come close to winning the Tour de France, he is a star. The trophies in his study, his ranking and his position as a team leader prove that.

Getting up from his chair to fetch another half grapefruit — "citrus fruits," he said, "they definitely fight cancer" — he barely looked at a prospectus for the next Tour de France that a friend had brought him.

"I think very little about that, maybe a quarter of the time," Armstrong said. "The other three quarters are focused on my life and beating cancer. If, for some reason, I can never race again, listen, that's fine."

The 1997 Tour would be extremely mountainous, not always Armstrong's favorite terrain, and, he was told jokingly, would be a terrible Tour for him.

"Cancer is a terrible Tour for me," he responded. "The Tour de France, it doesn't matter. You know.

"I would love to race but nothing's going to make me happier than to live. Life is the No. 1 priority. Professional cycling is No. 2. No, to create awareness for testes cancer is No. 2. Professional cycling is No. 3.

"I would like to create a foundation for awareness of testes cancer. I'd rather not have it but I've learned a lot about myself, about others and about life that most people never learn."

Did he feel it was unjust that he had cancer?

"No, because cancer doesn't play like that," he answered. "It doesn't play fair — nobody wants cancer. You can say, 'Why me?' but why not me? It doesn't strike because you've done something or not done something. I was just one of the ones it happened to hit.

"No, I don't want to waste my time saying, 'Why me?' I have a problem and I want to fix it."

Bits and Scraps

REMEMBER ANTHONY LANGELLA? He was the young *stagiaire* who sat in the front of the Gan team car as it headed to the Grand Prix d'Isbergues and listened to Michel Laurent's advice to stay alert. When he finished his brief time with Gan, Langella returned to his amateur team, CC Marmande, and had a bang-up season in 1996, finishing as the first amateur in the Grand Prix des Nations, taking second place in the French time-trial championship, second place in the Tour de la Corrèze, fifth place in the Tour of Japan, and 12th place in the world championship amateur time trial. He so highly impressed the Gan management this time that when the Tour de France passed through Bordeaux, where he lives, he was signed to a professional contract for 1997. Good luck, kid.

Cyril Sabatier, who sat in the rear seat of that team car, was less fortunate. He did turn pro in 1996, finding a berth with the Aki team in Monaco, but failed to make any sort of showing in his races. Perhaps he had the usual problems of the first-year pro — the races are so much longer and faster than they are at the amateur level — and perhaps he would begin to emerge in 1997.

By the end of the season, the best that many riders could do was look ahead to the next one.

Tony Rominger was signed for one more year, joining Cofidis as its leader and Lance Armstrong's replacement. A season that began with such bright hopes — maybe, finally, that elusive victory in the Tour de France — ended with his record showing as its highlights a victory in the Tour of Burgos in Spain, and third place in the Vuelta and the world championship time trial. Otherwise, nada.

Andy Hampsten, the same. He had a middling Tour of Switzerland and announced in the fall that he would retire. "After 12 very rewarding years as a pro, it's now time to concentrate fulltime on a lifetime contract with my family," he said. "If my racing has inspired, motivated or just given a grin to any fellow cyclists, I'll be very content." His team, U.S. Postal Service, bulked up for a European presence by hiring Slava Ekimov from Rabobank, Jean-Cyril Robin from Festina, Adriano Baffi from Mapei, and George Hincapie from Motorola, adding Johnny Weltz, Motorola's assistant *directeur sportif*, as the man behind the wheel of the team car.

Chris Boardman recuperated from the disappointment of the Tour and a bronze medal in the Olympic time trial by winning the world championship in pursuit, and then recapturing the world record for the hour. He clocked a superb 56.375 kilometers, or 1.084 farther than Rominger had traveled in 1994, and 4.105 than Boardman himself had gone in 1993.

On a rainy course, however, it was Alex Zülle who won the world championship time trial as Boardman played it just safe enough to finish second. Although Zülle also won the Vuelta, he was unable to collect enough points to move up from second place in the computerized standings ahead of Jalabert.

Miguel Arroyo, a true survivor, all 5 foot 5 inches of him, outlasted the shipwreck of ForceSud, which occurred without notice early in the summer, and resurfaced to join Aubervilliers 93, which lost Cyril Saugrain, the Tour stage winner, to Cofidis. Another survivor, Daisuke Imanaka, missed the winning break in the Japan Cup classic that ended the World Cup year, but still managed to get 12th place on home soil.

Finally, the smallest of notices that Casino–C'est Votre Equipe had signed a contract with a new team in the second division, EC St. Etienne Loire, to make it Casino's farm team. "A talent reservoir," Vincent Lavenu said, thinking big, as always. Milan–San Remo! Liège–Bastogne–Liège! The Tour de France!